REALITIES OF THE NEW CREATION

Rhema for You

A MENTALITY REVOLUTION

Glovis E. Eben

Volume One

DEDICATION

✝

This book is dedicated firstly to our Savior and Lord Jesus Christ for the wisdom that He continues to reveal to me through the Holy Spirit in the Word. Also to my parents Rev. John and Justina Eben who brought me up in the Word of God and taught me to pursue the call of God on my life. I would also like to dedicate this book to Pastor Chris Oyakhilome who has been an inspiration to me and helped me fall in love with the Word. I also dedicate this book to my beloved siblings (Melvies, Emmanuel, Pearl-Ruth, and Blessing), friends, and all those who pray for me and support the calling of God on my life.

KEYS FOR BIBLE
TRANSLATIONS USED

✝

KJV-King James Version

AMP-Amplified Version

NLT-New Living Translation

NIV-New International Version

MSG-Message Bible

NCV-New Century Version

CONTENTS

✝

Introduction

✝

Firstly, I would like to thank the Lord for revealing these divine inspirations to me and giving me the grace to be able to put them in writings. My intentions for sharing these precious, simple, yet very authentic words from the Spirit of God, is for you to be inspired and come into a realization of who you are. In 2007, God laid it on my heart to write a book. Still unsure about when and how I was going to go about this vision, for two years I did nothing regarding the book that God had spoken to me about. But by the grace of God, near August 2009, I received an idea from the Lord to send out encouraging messages and insights from the Scripture and the words I received from the Holy Spirit. My interest was in these believers becoming stronger in their walk with God. I soon realized that God wanted me to put these messages together in a book so that believers from all over the world could use them. These messages are to help believer understand their now-new life in Christ. I call it, *Realities of the new creation: Rhema for you.* This book will improve your spiritual life, and your understanding of the truths *(realities)* of the Word of God.

As you have already noticed, the sub-title of this book is *Rhema for You.* The written words of the Bible are called the *Logos* of God's Word. In other words, *Logos* are the words you see, read and hear. But the word that jumps up from the *logos* to your spirit is called *Rhema.* It is the insight or inspiration of the *Logos. Rhema* is the divine understanding of God's Word; the wisdom of God in action. It is prophetic, specific, and ushers God's power into your world-a word pregnant with God's anointing *(power and ability to effect change)* See Hebrews 4:12 (KJV).

It is not a word spoken out or given by mistake or by error; it is what I refer to as *a word-on-target.* This is what Jesus meant when he said, *"...the words that I speak unto you, they are spirit, and they are life" John 6:63 KJV.* In essence, He was saying, 'the words that I speak unto you are *Rhema'. Rhema* is food for the New Creation. It is that word of the Spirit, given by the Spirit, to effect a change in your life and situation. One *Rhema* word from God will turn your life right-side-up and embellish your life forever. A *Rhema* word will activate your faith and release power to produce the results you desire. It gives you a deeper understanding to what God has said, so that you may boldly say it. See Hebrews 13:5-6 (KJV). When you've got Rhema, your questions are answered and your doubts dissolved. The Word of God becomes real to your spirit and you boldly declare it unwaveringly.

Rhema for You, is not for the angels or unbelievers, but designed and inspired just for you. These revelations from the Word of God are for those who are born-again. They cannot be revealed to the world: for they are spiritually discerned. The Bible says in *1 Corinthians 2:14 KJV* that *"But the natural man receiveth not the things of the Spirit of God: for they are foolishness unto him: neither can he know them, because they are spiritually discerned."* It says here that the natural man [those who are not born-again] cannot receive *Rhema* because it is foolishness to him, and he cannot know them because they are spiritually discerned. It is the Holy Spirit that translates these mysteries to the understanding of the one who is born-again. But with the Holy Spirit, the world cannot have access to these divine truths.

The Bible says,

"⁶Howbeit we speak wisdom among them that are perfect [mature]: yet not the wisdom of this world, nor of the princes of this world, that come to nought: ⁷But we speak the wisdom of God in a mystery, even the hidden wisdom, which God ordained before the world unto our glory: ⁸Which none of the princes of this world knew: for had they known it, they would not have crucified the Lord of glory. ⁹But as it is written, Eye hath not seen, nor ear heard, neither have entered into the heart of man, the things which God hath prepared for them that love him.¹⁰But God hath revealed them unto us by his Spirit: for the Spirit searcheth all things, yea, the deep things of God" 1 Corinthians 2:6-10 KJV.

This is a powerful portion of Scripture! These mysteries [Rhema] were hidden from the princes of this world and according to *verse eight*, if they had known this wisdom; they would not have crucified Christ. You see, even angels were not allowed to have this information because it wasn't given to them. What do they need it for? But it has been given to us so we might know the deeper things of God. Hallelujah! No wonder Jesus said in the *Matthew 13:11 KJV*, *"He answered and said unto them, because it is given unto you to know the mysteries of the kingdom of heaven, but to them it is not given."*

My primary purpose in this book is to allow believers to get a deeper and more accurate understanding of God's Word so they can experience the power therein. This book is aims to help many Christians become more effective and efficient in their walk with God. Many Christians find the Bible to be confusing and difficult to read. However, in this book I attempt to break down and simplify certain scriptural concepts to dissolve confusions and contradictions one may have about the Bible. I believe that with the help of the Holy Spirit, this book will be of great impact to you.

Every excerpt will keep you focused on specific truths from God's Word which will build, encourage, correct, direct, instruct and inspire you. My desire for you dear reader, is that as you read these dynamic words from the Spirit, you'll become loaded with words that will not just last in you for a day or a short while, but for a lifetime. Each excerpt in this book is full of power that will literally change your life and your mentality. Therefore, I prescribe that you allow these words from each excerpt to completely whet your consciousness and settle in your spirit. Do not speed read through it, or read it like just another novel. Take time to constantly and frequently meditate on each excerpt and put every word into practice and watch it yield tangible results for you. You can also read *Realities of the new creation: Rhema for you,* over and over again to be well seasoned with the information you have gotten. This powerful material will not only address your spiritual affairs, but it will also extend to the physical, educational, emotional, material and financial aspects of your life. The message in this book is based on the Scriptural truths in the Word of God. Again, let the Holy Ghost minister to you as you read each excerpt. I am confident that this book will provoke growth in all areas of your life, catapult you into greater levels and help you live a life of excellence in Christ.

This book of revelations will modify and metamorphose every area of your life. Realities of the New Creation: *Realities of the New Creation* is rhema for you and a mentality revolution! I pray that the Holy Spirit will enlighten the eyes of your understanding to be able to believe, accept, proclaim and put to work these words in your life. Get ready for a life changing experience as you read and follow these inspiring words from the Spirit. Please do not fail to bless someone else with the messages you receive from this book for you are inspired to inspire and blessed to be a blessing. Thank you, keep shining and remain a blessing. With great pleasure, I present, Realities of the New Creation: *Rhema for you.*

EXCERPT 1

How to be Consistent

✝

Hello! One day, while in prayer I desperately asked the Lord, "how can I be consistent in my walk with you?" He said to me "in order to be consistent, you must <u>eliminate distractions.</u>" In order words, inconsistency is as a result of distractions. Upon hearing that, it became apparent that I had a lot of distractions in my life. These distractions made me very unstable as a Christian because I wasn't spending time to fellowship with the Word and the Holy Spirit like I should have. I was working, going to school and also spending too much time with friends. My busy lifestyle plus distractions, gave room for more problems. For the record, I'm not in any way insinuating that going to work, school or having fun with your friends are negative things. But when they've become your focus and you realize that you're love for God or for the things of God isn't growing, then, it is possible that you are being distracted by them. Basically, you know you are being distracted when you <u>set</u> your affections more on earthly things, and not on things above [Colossians 3:2 KJV]. There are too many distractions in the world today and these distractions must not veer us off the truth that we are here for a purpose and that we are pilgrims in this world.

Like I previously stated, inconsistency is as a result of distractions. I have realized that inconsistency is a problem for many believers today because of the distractions we entertain. The truth of the matter is, as long as we are in this world we will always encounter distractions, but we must never entertain them. In Matthew 4:11, we see that Jesus also had distractions in His life too and throughout His earthly ministry. One time, they wanted to make Him king [John 6:14-15] but He stayed consistent because He knew who He was and what He was called to do. Jesus is our perfect example of how not to entertain distractions. When you are unsure of who you are and what God has called you to do, chances are you will have major problems with distractions and become very inconsistent. Therefore, you must constantly search the scriptures to find out who you are and ask the Holy Spirit to reveal to you what you are called to do.

When you are consistent, you have your focus on what God has called you to do and you are following the guidance of the Word and the Spirit to accomplish it—you walk in accordance to God's plan and purpose. So many Christians are either way behind God's schedule or way ahead. But a consistent fellow is always on schedule with God. Consistency has a vital part to play in the growth of every believer. When you are inconsistent, you delay growth in your life. As a Christian, when you are not consistent you limit yourself from achieving more for God. It would behoove you to realize that God has no limit for your life.

One of the chief reasons many Christians become inconsistent is because of procrastination. Procrastination is the brother of inconsistency. The two are in the same family. When you procrastinate a lot in your walk with God or anything in life, it is likely that you will also become inconsistent. For example, if God asks you to do something before the end of the year, and the year ends without you doing it, you can expect to be inconsistent the next year. Think about it. If you are not doing what God wants you to do, anything else you do besides that becomes a distraction. So as long as you keep procrastinating, that's how long you are being distracted. Read the story of Jonah in Jonah 1-3 to get a better idea.

In addition, If you keep telling God you will do it later when He wants you to do it now, you'll most likely end up being inconsistent. You see dear friend, God is your life, and if you put God in the back seat; you're putting your life in the back seat. As a Christian, you must have already established the fact that God comes first before any other thing. Too many Christians put off the things of God (such as studying the Word, spending quality time with God, attending church activities) for the concerns of this world. Friend, you can't make progress as a Christian if you continue this way. Be proactive in your walk with God. Don't wait for your own time; be determined to please God and not yourself or anyone else. If you are struggling to read the Bible or how to even get started, relax, there is a whole excerpt on this ahead.

As I said from the beginning, to be consistent you must eliminate distractions. You cannot allow distractions in your life and expect to be consistent. It doesn't work that way. In order for you to eliminate distractions in your life and become more consistent, here are a few things that you will need to consider;

1. **We must always have the desire to grow.** *Lack of the desire to grow is like planting a seed without watering. If you want to be more consistent in any area of your life, it always starts, first, with a desire; a desire to move from your present level to the next. You say "Well how can I have the desire to grow?" Well I don't believe that anyone doesn't want to improve or do better than where they are. Everyone would like to become better and excel in any area of life. So, simply hate stagnation and believe you can always do better than your present stage. This will help you to have the desire to grow. When you have a constant desire to grow and do better, it motivates you to keep doing the right things to get to that next level. And when you stay motivated to do better, you'll hardly have any room for distractions.*

2. **Train your spirit to respond to God's Word quickly.** *In other words, don't waste time to respond to (do, obey or apply) God's Word when it's needed. Don't think or reason yourself out of it; do it immediately! Not responding to God's word immediately creates an opening for procrastination to set in, and eventually distractions. Do the Word without hesitancy and distractions won't find a place in you.*

3. **Talk Consistency.** *This means, always speak of what you need to do right or what you need to be consistent in doing and not what you have been doing wrong. Do not allow negative communication to come out of your mouth. For example, if you want to be consistent*

in reading your Bible and praying, don't say things like, "I always get bored when I read my Bible or fall asleep when I try to pray" When you talk like that, how can you have the desire to read your Bible or pray next time. If you have this problem, firstly, you'll find why and what to do in a later excerpt and what to do. Secondly, even though you see this is as a problem, if you are going to change it, you must talk contrary to how you feel. I venture to tell you that if you will begin saying things like, "I love the Word of God, it is my life, it shows me how I ought to live and produces in me what it talks about" and "My prayers mean a lot to God, He anticipates hearing my voice each day and when I pray big things happen." Even if you don't mean it, give it a few days, I assure you, you will not only mean it, but also begin to experience strength and joy rising up within you to read your Bible and pray consistently. Speak Consistency!

4. **Start and end each day meditating on the Word of God and praying.** *I also recommend praying in tongues. There will be more on meditation and praying in tongues in a later excerpt. This will stir up your spirit and keep you aware of your spirit life and you will not be carried away by things that are not beneficial.*

The scripture says, **"Quench not the Spirit"** 1 **Thessalonians 5:19 KJV.** This means you should not put the things of the Spirit to rest. Continue to stir up your spirit and keep it responsive to the will of God for your life. I urge you by the grace of God to develop a consistency mentality and be conscious of your spirit life.

Supporting Scripture(s):

Therefore, my beloved brethren, be ye steadfast [be firm, constant and consistent], unmovable, always abounding in the work of the Lord, forasmuch as ye know that your labor is not in vain in the Lord. 1 Corinthians 15:58 KJV

EXCERPT 2

Get the Word into your Spirit

✝

Hello! As food gives nourishment to keep your physical body active, even so, the Word of God gives nourishment to the spirit to keep it active and sustain it. Many times when we read God's Word, we read it only to the point where it reaches just the mind realm. The truth is the mind is not the only thing that needs to be full of the Word of God; the spirit (the spirit man) needs to be full too. The reason many believers wonder why reading the Bible doesn't make any difference in their lives and are living defeated in their spiritual lives is because they only keep the Word of God in the mind realm. All they have are memories of scriptures that have not yet taken root in their spirit. However, the Word of God must enter into your spirit if you are going to be changed by it or see the life changing results that it brings. In James 1:22, James talks about not being hearer only but also doers of the Word. This is because a hearer only lets the Word into his mind only, but a doer allows the Word into his heart [spirit]. Remember man is a spirit, he lives in a body and he has a soul. Since the real you is your spirit, if the Word of God will effect a change in you, it must reach you [your spirit], then, from your spirit to your soul and evidently your physical body. Change truly is from the inside out. Beloved, reading God's Word goes beyond merely getting the knowledge of it; every word you read from the Bible must soak your spirit. That is what brings change in your life! The Bible says in *Psalm 119:130 KJV* that, *"The entrance of thy words giveth light; it giveth understanding to the simple."* The question is, entrance into where? Into your spirit! For the light of God to shine in you and through you, the Word of God must enter and settle in you. Having the Word of God as a memory verse or a Bible story in your memory is not good enough for spiritual growth. With the Word in your spirit, you will gain mastery over your flesh and become a success in every area of your life.

The Bible says in *Hebrews 4:12 NIV, "For the word of God is living and active. Sharper than any double-edged sword, it penetrates even to dividing soul and spirit, joints and marrow; it judges the thoughts and attitudes of the heart."* You can only know the Word is living and active, when it has taken root in your spirit. You can't know it's living and active if it's only in your mind. The Word of God can only come alive in your spirit. Then, it will produce for you what it talks about. Glory to God!

"This book of the law shall not depart out of thy mouth; but thou shalt <u>meditate</u> therein day and night, that thou mayest observe to do according to all that is written therein: for then thou shalt make thy way prosperous, and then thou shalt have good success." Joshua 1:8 KJV

In the scripture above, notice that I underlined the word "meditate". A good definition of "<u>meditate</u>" is *a contemplation of spiritual matters.* Contemplation has to do with having a thoughtful observation, deliberation, and reflection with the concentration of your mind and your soul. This is how to get the Word into your spirit.

The Hebrew word for meditation is the word **"Hagah"** which means "to ponder, to mutter and also to roar." Hence, these are the three levels of meditation.

To ponder:-In the first level of meditation, you are quietly reading the scripture and visualizing it in your mind. At this point the Holy Spirit is making meaning of what you are reading. In other words, He is giving you an understanding of the passage you are reading.

To mutter:-The next level of meditation, this is when the Word rises from your thoughts to your lips. At this level you read it over and over to yourself in order to retain it; it becomes personal to you. It has moved beyond words written on pages-it becomes rhema to you. You are now aware that God is speaking to your situation, your questions are being answered and your doubts are being dissolved. This rhema word is for you a word-on-target, speaking to your condition and the circumstances you are presently encountering. It's so specific; you know God is talking to you, because the timing is just too right for it not to be God speaking. You no longer see it as the writings of Paul, Peter, and John etc. You put your name right there because it's talking to you, about you. Hallelujah!

To roar:-Finally, in the third level of meditation, you speak the word [rhema] out loud! Hopefully, there's no one around for you to disturb or be distracted by. So you roar like a lion saying that you are what God has said you are, you have what God has said you have and you can do what God has said you can do. Declaring aloud and boldly the rhema you've received from the Word over your life or situation. You'd sense by this time that what you were reading has taken root in your spirit.

These three levels of meditation, is how you get the Word into your spirit.

Study God's Word till your spirit becomes saturated and overwhelmed by it, so that it can come alive in you. God's Word must settle in your spirit and become part of you. In fact, study it until you become that Word! For example, if you are studying a verse that says, "By His stripes you are healed" See Isaiah 53:5 (KJV). Do not only have just the memory or knowledge of that verse, meditate on it, until you become the healing it's talking about. When you meditate on the Word, it produces the result you desire and makes you one with it. Meditating on the Word makes you one with the Word. When you meditate on the fact that you are healed by the stripes of Jesus, if you needed healing, it will rise in you from your spirit to your body. Much more, you will become one with the healing virtue, and if anyone around you needed a healing, if they even mistakenly bump into you, that healing anointing will transfer from you to them.. So much so that wherever you go, no sickness or infirmity can stand your presence. This is to say, the Word has become flesh. You are now a living healing body. Hallelujah!

You may ask, "Pastor, could this be real?" Emphatically Yes! Think about Jesus and the numerous healings and miracles He performed on people during His earthly ministry. Could he have healed them if He was not one with healing? I believe you can't give what you don't have. Don't separate the healing from the Healer; they are one! Remember He is I AM. In order words, I AM whatever you need. If you need healing I AM, if you need provision, I AM, if you need strength, I AM. I AM whatever you need me to be for you! You see, as He is, so are we in this world [1 John 4:17]. Jesus is the Head, and we are His body. That's why we are called the body of Christ. Therefore, those things Jesus was able to do when He was on earth, even though He is in Heaven, He is still doing it through His body, for the Head and the body are ONE! You say, "Isn't that making yourself like Jesus?" That's exactly my point! You are one with Him and the Glory that the He has, you have. Read the prayer Jesus prayed to His Father in John 17:21-23. This prayer was answered after His resurrection and when you get born-again. You are now exactly like your Elder Brother Jesus. Hallelujah!

The apostles were conscious of this reality. It is no wonder that they accomplished great things for God and walked miraculously like they did. The Bibles says from the Apostle Paul's clothes were taken handkerchiefs and aprons, and as they were placed on the sick they were healed [Acts 19:12]. What about the Apostle Peter's shadow healing the sick [Acts 5:15]. I don't know about you, but this is enough evidence that when you meditate on the Word long enough, you become one with that word and that just as Jesus who was the Word was made flesh [John 1:1-2], the Word of God in your spirit also becomes flesh. I like what Peter said to the man at the gate called beautiful in Acts 3, **"such as I have, give I unto thee"**, but now, much more, **"such as I am, give I unto thee."** Glory to God! This is the power and beauty of meditating on God's Word. It must become flesh or one with you [your spirit]. I challenge you to allow God's Word to reside in your spirit and make you what it talks about.

Supporting Scripture(s):

Thy word have I hid in mine heart [spirit], that I might not sin

against thee.

Psalms 119:11 KJV

EXCERPT 3

The Best Teacher

✝

Hello! It has been said that *Experience* is the best teacher, but I believe that in our case as the New Creation in Christ, the *Holy Spirit* is our best teacher. I understand that we learn from our experiences and the experiences of others. Howbeit, as people of God with the Spirit of God in us, we function by the Spirit. Many times, we wait for something bad to happen before we learn from it. It's sad how many Christians rely only on their experiences rather than relying on the Holy Spirit to teach them. Beloved, this is the system of the world, it is not so for the Believer in Christ. We don't wait to learn from our experience, we learn from the Holy Spirit through the Word. The *Holy Ghost* is our primary teacher not *Experiences.*

> But the Comforter (<u>*Counselor,*</u> *Helper, Intercessor, Advocate, Strengthener, Standby), the Holy Spirit, Whom the Father will send in my name [in my place, to represent me and act on my behalf], <u>He will teach you all things</u>. And He will cause you to recall (will remind you of, bring to your remembrance) everything I have told you. John 14:26 AMP*

There are two things I want you to see in the scripture above. Firstly, I'd like you to see that the Holy Spirit is referred to as *the Counselor.* Counselor means teacher, trainer, or strategist. Therefore, the Holy Spirit is our extraordinary strategist-the one who gives us *divine strategies* for living. Everything we need to know about our lives and life in general, He makes them known to us. Secondly, what makes the Holy Spirit a far better counselor or teacher than *experience* is the next thing we see underlined in that scripture. He is a better teacher than experience because He *teaches us <u>all</u> things.* Experience teaches you *some* things **not** *all* things. But the Holy Spirit will break everything down for you. He is the *Master Teacher* to the Christian. It is important for you to learn first from the Holy Spirit and not have gone through 'experience' before you can learn a lesson. Allow the Holy Spirit to teach you. He is more than well rounded.

The Word says, *"He teaches you all things."* Well, I figured if He teaches all things, this mean He knows all things. See why as a Christian you can't fail? You have the BEST Teacher who knows all things. Praise God! May be you're a student, and you're not doing well in a particular course; if you will yield to the Holy Spirit in you, I can assure you that He will teach you and help you to understand the course better. Take advantage of this *Wonderful Teacher*, and you'd be amazed at the results you will produce.

Some of the other benefits you enjoy when you allow the teaching ministry of the Holy Spirit to be at work in your life is that the things we learn from Him are always accurate, complete, and come with clarity. You cannot be confused or uncertain about what He teaches you. His teachings will help you know the right moves to make in any given situation.

However, you cannot learn from the Holy Spirit or know when He is teaching you, if you are not studying the Word. The Holy Spirit doesn't just teach you anything outside of God's Word; what He teaches you will always be in line with the Word. As you get yourself acquainted with God's Word, it even begins to help you understand *how* the Holy Spirit teaches you. Don't wait for an experience; be expedient with the Holy Spirit. In other words, take advantage of the teaching and training given to you by the Spirit of God.

I encourage you by the mercies of God to yield yourself to the teaching and direction of the Spirit of God because what you get from Him is better than what you learn from any experience.

Supporting Scripture(s):

[13]*But when He, the Spirit of Truth (the Truth-giving Spirit) comes, He will guide you into [teach you] all the Truth (the whole, full Truth). For He will not speak His own message [on His own authority]; but He will tell whatever He hears [from the Father; He will give the message that has been given to Him], and He will announce and declare to you the things that are to come [that will happen in the future].*[14]*He will honor and glorify Me, because He will take of (receive, draw upon) what is Mine and will reveal (declare, disclose, transmit) it to you. John 16:13-14 AMP*

EXCERPT 4

Remember to 'Say'

✞

Hello! The Bible says, "*... If ye have faith as a grain of mustard seed, ye shall say unto this mountain, Remove hence to yonder place; and it shall remove; and nothing shall be impossible unto you*" *Matthew 17:20 KJV*. Often times when we read this verse, our attention is drawn to just the fact that if our faith is like the size of a mustard seed, it will move mountains. As beautiful as that is, let's take a look into the whole verse properly. Faith is a definite requirement to move mountains in our lives; however, according to this scripture, it is not the only necessary ingredient for moving mountains. If you look at this verse closely, you will notice the phrase "*ye shall say*." These three words are not to be ignored. As faith is vital in moving mountains, so is the *say*. Faith alone will not move the mountains in your life, you must *say* [speak] unto the mountains as well.

You may have faith that God can take away that problem or obstacle in your life, but you still need to activate your faith by speaking to that problem (mountain) and tell it to move. Like a chemical reaction, speech is the catalyst that activates your reaction or the movement of the mountain. The two ingredients are inactive until you combine them. Learn to speak to your mountains because until you tell them to move, they will stay there. Don't expect your faith alone to get the job done; you must do the "say" too. This is very important for you to know and understand. Take for example, a bulldozer cannot bring down buildings without its controller or conductor; likewise faith is ineffective without the "say"! Your faith represents a bulldozer and what you *say* (your words of faith) represents the controller. Therefore, use your faith and your words of faith to bring down those obstacles you face. It is important to have faith, but God wants you to verbalize your faith.

Paul the Apostle says in 2 Corinthians 4:13 (KJV) *"We having the same spirit of faith, according as it is written, I believed, and therefore have I spoken; we also believe, and therefore speak"* In other words, people know what you believe because you speak it forth. Faith Speaks! It is not quiet. For instance, if you are feeling sick and you believe that God has healed you, don't go on telling people how sick you are or how much pain you feel. Back your faith with your "say" and say you're healed, and don't talk sickness. The speaking part of faith should not be ignored. Declare [announce] what you believe.

"For verily I say unto you, that whosoever shall <u>say</u> unto this mountain, Be thou removed, and be thou cast into the sea; and shall not thou in his heart; but shall <u>believe</u> that those things which he <u>saith</u> shall come to pass; he shall have whatsoever he <u>saith</u>." Mark 11:23 (KJV). If you pay close attention to the verse we just read, you'd discover something beautiful that the Spirit of God is trying to bring across to us. Notice in this verse, the "saying" is mentioned three times and the "believing" once. I believe the Holy Spirit through the writer St. Mark is letting us know that we are supposed to "say" three times more than we "believe". In essence, the "saying" is three times more important than the "believing." They are *both* needed to move those mountains in your life. Therefore, learn to speak out what you already believe. Keep saying it; don't stop talking it! For example, if you believe that God has healed you of that condition, start saying you are well. The truth of the

matter is, you are well, you are not sick, because by His stripes you were healed [1 Peter 2:24]. If you believe you are healed; say it out. It doesn't matter if the pain is still there. Don't change your confession of healing and refuse to recognize the presence of your pain. You'll soon discover that the sickness and its symptoms have given up on your body. Glory to God! This will also work for your finances, your marriage, your children, your job and all other areas of your life.

Your *faith* and what you *say* will determine the result you get. Faith alone doesn't move your mountains until you speak. Speak out your faith every day over your life and bring those things you desire to pass. I charge you by the Spirit of God to be more verbal with your faith and call forth those things that are not as though they were.

Supporting Scripture(s):

That the communication of your faith may become effectual by the acknowledging of every good thing which is in you in Christ Jesus.

Philemon 1:6 (KJV)

EXCERPT 5

Might-divine ability

✠

Hello! As you study God's Word carefully, you'll find out that God has given us (the believer) the ability (*might*) to do the right things. This divine ability is called *Might*. The Greek rendering for *Might* is *Dunamis [power, strength, ability]*. This is what I called *spiritual momentum*. The Word of God declares, *"Finally, be strong in the Lord and in the power of His might"* Ephesians *6:10 KJV*. You can only stay strong in the Lord and in all the things God has called you to do when *His might* is working in you. The Lord says "be strong" because He knows that you will have times where you'll face difficulties in doing the right things. The good news is that we have the *might of God* available to us. Therefore, when we face these difficult moments and feel pressed to do the wrong things, we must realize that there is an inner ability available for us each day to live beyond struggles.

[29]He giveth power to the faint; and to them that have no might he increaseth strength. [30]Even the youths shall faint and be weary, and the young men shall utterly fall: [31]But they that wait upon the LORD shall renew their strength; they shall mount up with wings as eagles; they shall run, and not be weary; and they shall walk, and not faint. Isaiah 40:29-31 KJV.

In the scripture above, it says to them that have no might God increase their strength. Therefore, even if you think you have no might to operate rightly as a Christian, God will increase your strength. In other words, you can never lack strength in your life to do the things of God. May be you have consistently found yourself doing the wrong things and you have found it difficult to stop that pattern of behavior, I want you to know that, within you, there is an ability to do the right thing. Be conscious of God's divine ability on the inside. Strength or might is inherent in the Believer. Nonetheless, if you must continue in His might, you must learn to wait on the Lord as said in the scriptures stated above. You wait on the Lord by spending time with the Lord, feeding yourself with the Word and having fellowship with other Believers. These three things will help stir up the *might* of God in you and cause you to stand strong every day.

You may be thinking that what you are struggling with is too hard for you to conquer. But I want you to know that the struggle is too small for you because God's strength is working mightily in you. Refuse to acknowledge the strength of your weakness and recognize the strength of your God in you. Remember, you can do all things through Christ *which* [not who] strengthens you. See Philippians 4:13 (KJV). So it is not referring to Christ the person, but Christ the anointing [power, might, ability], because in the Greek, the word *Christ* means both the *Anointed One* and *His Anointing*. Hence, if Christ be in you, you have the divine ability to do the right things with ease. With His might in you, you cannot be defeated! Even if you don't feel strong enough, just remember feelings aren't the reality. The reality is whatever the Word of God says about you. I encourage you by the grace of God to know that God's might is at work in you and by reason of His divine ability in you, know that His strength is made perfect in weakness.

Supporting Scripture(s):

⁹And he said unto me, my grace is sufficient for thee: for my strength is made perfect in weakness. Most gladly therefore will I rather glory in my infirmities, that the power of Christ may rest upon me. ¹⁰Therefore I take pleasure in infirmities, in reproaches, in necessities, in persecutions, in distresses for Christ's sake: for when I am weak, then am I strong. 2 Corinthians 12:9-10 KJV

EXCERPT 6

The blessings are already available

✝

Hello! Many times I've come across Christians who wonder why they are not being blessed. Although they pray countless times and fast, pay their tithes and do God's work faithfully, they wonder why they are still living from paycheck to paycheck and struggling all the time to make ends meet. Friend, permit me shock you a bit. *The blessings you seek are already available.*

You may be thinking, "If they really are already available, why am I not seeing it?" Beloved, the Word says, *"Blessed be the God and Father of our Lord Jesus Christ, who hath blessed us with all spiritual blessings in heavenly places in Christ" Ephesians 1:3 KJV.* Now, if God says He has blessed us with *all the blessings in heavenly places in Christ*, then, what other blessings are we asking for? He said, He has already blessed us with *all* that we need in Christ. This means, Christ is the embodiment of *all* the blessings you need or will ever need in your life. Therefore, if you have Christ in you, you have everything. You lack nothing! The question then becomes, how can one make these blessings work and manifest in his or her life?

Notice, in the scripture we read, the blessings are called *spiritual* blessings not *physical*. First, you must understand that there is a spiritual realm as well as a physical realm. In the realm of the spirit everything we need or will ever need has already been made available to us. However, it is the responsibility of every Christian to make that transfer from the spiritual realm into the natural realm. This is the reason God wants you to ask is because He already made it available. He won't tell you to ask for something if He hasn't already made available. If it wasn't already available, there will be no need for asking. God has blessed us with all spiritual blessings in heavenly places in Christ. When you know that all that you need has already been made available, you are not afraid to ask. You don't feel unworthy to have what you are asking for and you know it's God's will for you to have it. If God didn't want you to have it, He wouldn't have blessed you with *all* spiritual blessings in the first place.

Therefore, now that you know you have these blessings already, spiritually, your responsibility is to make a transfer from the spiritual to the physical manifestation of these blessings. The problem with many Christians is that we tend to operate in with a 'lack mentality" instead of a 'supply mentality'. With a 'lack mentality', you are conscious of what you don't have and complaining about it. So much so that even our prayers are full of complains and not really asking in faith. When you complain, you say things like, "God, why am I always broke, what did I do to deserve this pain?" "I can't take this anymore, I'm frustrated and confused with my life", "I'm not as good in school like my friends", "I wasn't born in a rich family and my parents were never there for me." Friend, complaining is not a form of prayer because it chokes up your faith. The reason a lot of Christians are broke and not experiencing a flow stream of blessings in their lives is because they haven't learnt God's principle of converting spiritual blessings to the physical domain.

Firstly, to make a transfer of spiritual blessings to the physical, you need to position yourself rightly. What do I mean by this? Imagine that a woman who is in need of a child and has been praying for the fruit of the womb, but, she is always cursing and mistreating the children of other women. Do you think she has positioned herself for the blessing of a child? I'm sure you would disagree. It may not even be something as big as that, it may be your attitude towards God and towards people that is limiting you from an extraordinary stream-flow of blessings. Positioning yourself rightly; it's practically releasing your faith. When you ask God for a child and show love to the children of other women, you are releasing your faith, because even though you don't have children of your own yet, you are developing the heart of a mother. Positioning yourself rightly is simply demonstrating faith toward that which you've asked for.

Blessings are not given; they are taken because they're yours already in Christ. Don't misquote me when I say blessings are not given. All blessings are from God. But He has already given us all spiritual blessings in His Son Jesus. The given part is already done, now the taking or receiving part is left for you. As we position ourselves rightly, we turn those spiritual blessings into the natural. So, how do you position yourself rightly? You do so by meditating on the Word of God, walking in the light of it and capitalizing by speaking the Word of God over your life and situation consistently.

When we are not walking in the light of God's Word by doing what it says, we tend to lose blessings instead of gaining blessings. It is imperative that we position ourselves rightly for God's supernatural flow of blessings. We don't need to struggle to be blessed; we are already blessed!

Secondly, always make declarations that you are blessed with all spiritual blessings in heavenly places and lay claims on them in the name of Jesus. Don't be conscious of what you lack; be conscious of the supply you already have in Christ and claim it. Stop making statements like "I'm suffering", "I'm broke", "I'm surviving" or "I'm hanging in there". The blessings of God can't flow in your life if you continually make negative statements like this. This kind of negative communication builds up walls between the spiritual realm and the natural realm, thus limiting a transfer. Don't talk contrary to what you already have spiritually. Even if you haven't seen the physical manifestation, talk in line with what you know is already available in the realm of the spirit. Learn to lay claim on what you already have available. If it's money that you require, instead of saying that you're broke, say that you are rich because He became poor. See 2 Corinthians 8:9 (KJV). Some will say "Pastor, isn't it being unrealistic to say you have something you cannot see?" Remember, faith is not the evidence of things **seen**, but the evidence of things **not seen**. If you can already see it, you won't need to ask for it because it's already there in the physical. You don't need to have faith for something you can see. But because it is still in the spiritual realm, and you require it in the physical realm, you simply declare what you see and know you have in the spiritual. Faith is calling real what is unreal to your sensory perception. Declaring and claiming what you want to see in the physical is still a demonstration of your faith and how you transfer spiritual blessings into physical. God has given us so many principles in His Word on how we can make this transfer and as you keep reading this book, I will explain a few more.

Another way to transfer spiritual blessings to the natural realm is by sowing seeds or being a radical giver. When you sow seeds and give to the work of God and to people, you literally make spiritual blessings manifest in the physical. Sowing also enables you to demonstrate or release your faith for what you want. The scripture says *Luke 6:38 KJV*, *"...give and it shall be given unto you good measure, press down, shaken together and running over shall men give unto thy bosom. For with the same measure you mete withal it shall be measure to you again."* The law of sowing and reaping works for everybody [believers and non-believers]. Yet, there are many Christians who are barely getting by in life because they've failed to recognize these principles of transfer. Do you feel like you work for years and never have anything to show for it, you are very prayerful and faithful in your walk with God, yet you still struggle a great deal? Beloved, this is not God's best for you; not with all that we have in Christ. Make up your mind to follow God's sowing principle of transfer. There is no telling the blessings that will flow into your life when you put this principle of sowing to work. It will yield immense results! See 2 Corinthians 9:6-8 (KJV, NLT, and AMP)

These are a few ways on how you will begin to see the blessings of God materialize in your life. I urge you to know that the blessings are already available and all you have to do is apply God's principles of conversion.

Supporting Scripture(s):

[21]Therefore let no man glory in men. <u>For all things are yours;</u>
[22]Whether Paul, or Apollos, or Cephas, or the world, or life, or death, or things present, or things to come; <u>all are yours;</u> [23]And ye are Christ's; and Christ is God's. 1 Corinthians 3:21-23 KJV

EXCERPT 7

Smile at your problems

✝

Hello! *"Every good gift and every perfect (free, large, full) gift is from above; it comes down from the Father of all [that gives] light, in [the shining of] Whom there can be no variation [rising or setting] or shadow cast by His turning [as in an eclipse]" James 1:17 AMP.*

A lot of times when we encounter difficulties in our lives, we tend to accuse or blame God for our misfortune, forgetting that God is NOT the author of the bad things that happens to us. A Christian, who makes statements like, "God allowed bad things to happen to me for a reason or God wants me to suffer because He wants to teach me something out of this", is somewhat ignorant of certain truths about God. Statements like these are tools that the enemy uses to keep God's people in bondage.

Beloved, God is not the author of your problems; He only desires to get you out of them. The scripture we just read says that *every good and every perfect gift comes from God.* It is as clear and as straightforward as can be. When you label God as the cause of your problems, it is impossible to see Him yet as the very solution to those problems. God is either the problem causer or the problem solver. He cannot be both. So which one do you believe He is to you?

You must understand that going through difficult times does not signify the absence of God, but rather the presence of the enemy trying to steal, kill and to destroy. However, the enemy can only attack you when you let him in. When you operate in fear and unbelief, no matter how small it may be, the devil capitalizes on it and causes problems for you. Therefore, when you face problems or difficult moments, be wise to never be moved by them by being anxious, complaisant and afraid. The solution to your problem existed long before the problem came. God has already given you the solution to every need or problem you have. It is inside you! Every problem gravitates towards the direction of its solution. You have the power as a believer to change your circumstances. The reason a lot believers suffer with the same issue for long is not because God is allowing it; it's actually because they are allowing it. This is so because God has given you authority of serpents and scorpions and over all the power of the enemy. Now that you have the power to change any circumstance, God is waiting on you to act on the authority you have received from Him. As a matter of fact, God allows what you allow. See Matthew 18:18 NCV. Hence, the blame should be on us, not God for allowing problems to stick around for too long. The truth is, problems will definitely show up in your life, but how long it stays there is up to you.

Also, it should not be a strange thing for a Christian to know that the devil is the agent behind problems. He is the author of every bad and imperfect gift. But like I said before, we, as believers are superior to Satan and his cohorts—we have the authority and dominion over their works. So when you face any problem, it is an opportunity for you to display the authority that you have over those circumstances that are tabled before you. Carrying on whining to God about the problems you have and all that you're going through will not get them solved. You must be bold against the enemy; use your authority in Christ against his evil works.

One very important sign of spiritual maturity of a believer is to *smile or laugh* whenever he encounters problems. This proves a strong confidence in God. It is also one of the quickest ways to release your faith in any situation. You smile or laugh at the face of adversity and act like they're unreal. The devil hates when you ignore him or whatever he is doing. He wants to be acknowledged for his wicked works. The reason many problems we have escalate to bigger problems is because those problems become all we ever talk about. I've noticed that believers tend to give the devil too much attention when bad things happen. For example, If you have a fever and go about telling everyone that you are sick, that is one way of acknowledging that the devil's work is actually succeeding in your body. Even if you know that the devil is the cause of the fever, only mention the fever when you are casting it out. You don't need the world to know that you are feeling feverish. You are only glorifying the activity of the devil in your body and instead of speaking life to the situation; you are only talking about it. You must learn to ignore what the devil is doing and maintain the confession of faith saying that you are the healed of the Lord and by the stripes of Jesus you are well. Remember the devil is a thief. He wants to steal your joy away. So when he brings problems to you expecting to make you unhappy and worried, but you still put a smile on your face and laugh, you put him in big confusion. Don't give in to your problems, smile and laugh when you encounter them and you will ignore them out of your life.

The Bible says in **Job 5:22 KJV, "At the face of destruction and famine you shall laugh..."** Not crying, complaining or blaming God for it, LAUGH! You say, "Should I just start laughing when nothing is funny?" Yes! Besides, the Christian does not laugh only when something is funny. The Word of God declares, *"When the Lord turned again the captivity of Zion, we were like them that dream. Then was our mouth filled with laughter and our tongue with singing..."* (Psalm 126:1-2 KJV). A lot of times we forget laughter and go unto singing. But *laughter* is important as well as singing. What then is *laughter* to a believer? *Laughter* is an expression of Victory! When you smile and laugh in the face of adversity, you let the devil know that you are sure of your victory even in that adverse situation.

The next time you are confronted with a problem, don't accuse God or blame him for it; just smile and say "thank you Lord for another opportunity to come out victorious." Halleluiah! Refuse to cry and whine about the problems in your life; smile and have dominion over them! Know that you are more powerful than your problems and bigger than your troubles. I charge you to not be dismayed about your problems or blame God for them, but to put on a big smile an act like they don't even exist.

Supporting Scripture(s):

[35] Who shall ever separate us from Christ's love? Shall suffering and affliction and tribulation or calamity and distress or persecution or hunger or destitution or peril or sword? [36] Even as it is written, for Thy sake we are put to death all the daylong; we are regarded and counted as sheep for the slaughter. [37] Yet amid all these things we are more than conquerors and gain a surpassing victory through Him who loved us.

Romans 8:35-37 AMP

EXCERPT 8

Understanding the Power of Words

✠

Hello! Did you know that the power of Life and Death is not in the hands of God nor the devil? This may sound strange to a religious mind, but it is the truth. The Scripture says, *"Death and Life are in the power of the tongue" Proverbs 18:21 (KJV)*. In other words, the power of *death* and *life* is in your words. What you say can either take you up or bring you down. God has put power in our tongue. We have been given the authority over the affairs of death or life; but it is unfortunate that many believers don't use this power to their advantage.

When God created the earth, He did not need to do anything extraordinary or special; He merely uttered words and everything came into its rightful place. You may be thinking, "Well that's God, He can do anything." Let me remind you of the Scripture my dear reader, the Bible says we are made in His image and in His likeness (Genesis 1:28 KJV); in His *image* because we look like Him, in His *likeness* because we function exactly like Him. Whatever He does, we can also do! You must discover the weight of power that lies in your tongue and make use of it.

Sometimes what we may be going through needs no prayers. There are some situations that only go by simple spoken words and no matter how much you pray, your situation doesn't change, especially with situations that have to do with demonic oppression. There is nowhere in the Bible that God ever asked us to consult Him about a demon spirit or a devil. He said to us in Mark 16:17-18 that we are to cast out devils, not pray to Him about them. How do you do it? The same way Jesus did it! Use simple spoken words of command.

You must realize that the devil himself and all the demons understand spiritual authority. But they seek to know if you [the believer] also understand your authority over them. For instance, you may have a devil of fever troubling you. That devil of fever understands that with the authority you have over him, you just need say, "Go" and the fever will leave. But if that devil notices that you are wasting all your energy on trying to bind, cast and loose, a little fever could eventually become malaria because you have not realized your authority over him. Mean while all you needed to solve that problem was to say one word, "Go". When you don't know these things, you will continually beg God for things instead of acknowledging and exercising the power and authority He has already given to you.

I believe the longest time Jesus ever spent casting out devils was less than thirty seconds. He didn't spend hours, only seconds! I hope that many ministers of the Gospel can understand that they too can operate in that dimension of authority. Jesus understood the power of His words. You have that same authority dear friend; so, begin to exercise it now.

In Matthew 8:5-10, there is the story of the centurion whose servant was sick of palsy and he came to Jesus to ask for His help. But when Jesus wanted to come to his house to heal the servant, the centurion told Jesus to just 'speak the word' and his servant will be healed. How powerful is that? This is a man in a place of authority; he understands the power of words. He knew from experience that all he had to say to his servants is 'go here' and they'll go, 'come here' and they'll come, 'do this' and they'll do it. The man figured Jesus had greater authority than himself. So he knew just by the word of the master, his servant will be healed. Dear friend, there is power in your spoken words! Therefore, sickness, sin, poverty, and whatsoever the evil one has sent against you will have no place in your life, if you understand the power of your words and use them well. What a life we have in Christ! Hallelujah!

The realm of the spirit is controlled by words and what you say here in the earth will determine what happens for you there in spiritual places. That's why Jesus said, **"...Man shall not live by bread alone, but by every word..." Matthew 4:4**. The kind of words you speak determines your living condition. What kind of words do you speak? Are they words of faith, power, life, health and success or words of fear, weakness, death, sickness and failure? Make your life full of the right words. Let your words be consistent with what God has said about you.

Your words carry more than enough power to change your life for good or for bad. Open your mouth and release those words of faith and watch God's power back every letter of every word that proceeds out of your mouth. When you release words of faith, they will come back with results. Let this stir up your faith and make you conscious of God's divine power in your mouth. I charge you by the power of God to learn how to use your *words* to rule your *world.*

Supporting Scripture(s):

For by thy words ye shall be justified, and by thy

words ye shall be condemn.

Matthew 12:37 KJV

EXCERPT 9

Ministry of reconciliation

✝

Hello! The Bible says that, *"...God has called us into a ministry of reconciliation" 2 Corinthians 5:18 KJV.* **A Farlex dictionary definition of the word reconciliation is, "getting two things to correspond".** When Christians don't talk or relate well with one another, their behavior defeats the purpose of what Christianity is all about. The scripture we just read says every one of us have been called into the ministry of reconciliation. We have been called by God to get any two things to correspond (work together, be in union, be in peace, and in harmony). In other words, not only are we meant to reconcile others together; we ourselves are to be in good terms with others. We have the responsibility of bringing love to our world, and repairing, restoring, and building bridges between families, friends, churches, communities and even nations. Sadly, many Believers walk contrary to this divine calling.

I've noticed when two people are at odds to the level in which they cease talking to one another, they wait for the each other to be the first to apologize and/or admit that they are wrong. This should not be the attitude of a child of God. Many times we allow pride to gain mastery over us which in turn causes us not to be on good terms with someone who may have offended us or someone we may have a misunderstanding with. When a Christian has this kind of attitude, he limits and resists the flow of the Spirit in his life. This is what I meant in *Excerpt 6* when I talked about being in the right position for the overflow of blessings. If you are a Christian with an unforgiving and prideful attitude, you shut up the heavens over your life. See 1 Peter 5:5 (KJV). This is why when some of us pray, it seems as though God is not listening to our prayers, and whereas the real problem lays within ourselves and the people in our lives that we refuse to relate with. These are the people that if we see them walking in our direction, we take another route or whatever they say, even if it's right, we disagree just because we are not on talking terms with them. Beloved, you cannot continue to live this way.

The Bible says that we should *"Follow [pursue] peace with all men, and holiness, without which no man shall see the Lord"* Hebrews *12:14 KJV.* The NIV says, *"Make every effort to live in peace with all men and to be holy; without holiness no one will see the Lord."* I wonder how many of us really follow the scriptures word for word. How much effort do you put in reconciling with a friend, a spouse, a co-worker, a neighbor, a parent, a classmate or whoever it may be? Do you wait for them to say "I'm sorry" first before you reconcile with them? Remember the scripture didn't say that you should wait for the person to say I'm sorry first before you reconcile but rather that you are called [ordained] to reconcile. That means reconciliation should be your lifestyle—something we do without restrain. The Christian doesn't wait for an apology to forgive, but rather, forgives because he himself has been forgiven. See Matthew 18:21-35 (KJV).

I pray that God will give you the desire to reconcile with people even when they don't show any effort to reconcile with you or apologize. When you make efforts to reconcile with people who may not even want to reconcile with you, it reveals the character and nature of God in you. Remember what Christ did for you, that even when we were yet sinners Christ died for us. See Romans 5:8 (KJV). This is so awesome! We didn't make any efforts to be reconciled to Him neither did we show any remorse for our wicked works, yet, Christ in His great love wherewith He loved us, came to die for us and forgave all our sins **(past, present and future)**. To find out more on forgiveness, I strongly recommend this wonderful book, *Destined to Reign* by Joseph Prince. The truth is **no one should ever deserve forgiveness; it is the work of grace [unmerited favor]**. So don't expect someone to do something deserving before you forgive him or her. Forgive because you have been called into the ministry of reconciliation and because you too have been forgiven all your sins. I encourage you by His grace to visit, call, or even take someone who you are not talking to out on a nice dinner and reconcile with him or her.

Supporting Scripture(s):

And become useful and helpful and kind to one another, tenderhearted (compassionate, understanding, loving-hearted), forgiving one another [readily and freely], as God in Christ forgave you. Ephesians 4:32 AMP

EXCERPT 10

Be a tough-minded Christian

✝

Hello! One vital reason many Christians who struggle with sin fall into diverse trials and temptations is because they are not tough-minded. So what does it mean to be tough-minded? It means to have an undefeated mind; the mind of a winner, a mind that is not easily deceived and does not compromise.

I've heard many Christians say that it's difficult for them to give up their will or self-pleasure to please God. They believe that being a Christian is hard and a struggle, because they would have to give up some personal pleasure. When you do not have complete understanding of what Christianity is all about, you may be led to believe that this is the right way of thinking.

No Christian can be effective or efficient in their walk without mental toughness. This is not will-power; it is an ability of your born-again spirit you must become fully conscious of. It is revealed as steadfastness, perseverance or longsuffering. For the battle of life is carried out in the realm of the mind. What God wants for you as a Christian, is for you to be tough-minded—to have a mind that is unafraid, not easily discouraged, and a mind that is set on God's Word. The scripture says in **2 Timothy 1:7 KJV, "For God hath not given us the spirit of fear; but of power, and of love, and of a sound mind."** Friend, you need to live completely conscious of this truth every day! God has given you a sound mind! This is a mind that is disciplined and aptly acts on God's will. It does not give in to temptations or show weakness in times of trials and tribulation; it is completely alert and focused on the Word of His grace.

Also, a tough minded Christian does not allow guilt, shame and condemnation to dominion over his mind. He is always righteousness-conscious! Many Christians are being overwhelmed with guilt and condemning thoughts or feelings because there are weak-minded. When you are weak-minded, you believe every lie the devil tells you and allow fear and worries to rule you. From today, make a conscious decision to be tough-minded by giving rapt attention to God's word.

Being tough-minded is not just about being able to stand the test of time or standing strong when tempted, it is also about not giving up when you do fall or allowing the devil to make you feel unworthy because of a sin you committed, but picking yourself up, believing that you are still loved by God and that you can do better next time. As a Christian, you are built to overcome every sin, trial, temptation and every difficulty you encounter. And even if you fall or do something wrong, you must be tough-minded in knowing and being confident of the fact that you are still in right standing with God. You've got to stand strong and be tenacious in the things of God and not allow your mind to be weakened by oppressive thoughts. As Paul told Timothy in 2 Timothy 2:1; friend, I say to you today, stand strong in the grace which is in Christ Jesus.

Remember the mind is a battleground for good versus evil. Therefore, you must be mentally tough; otherwise, you will let the operation of evil gain mastery over the operation of good in your mind and subsequently in your life. Jesus is a great example of someone who was very resilient and demonstrated tough-mindedness. When you study the book of Matthew 4, you'll see how Jesus Christ maintained a tough-mind despite the very persuasive temptations presented before Him by the devil. He was able to overcome the devil by using the Word of God. Even when tempted by the Pharisees, Sadducees and Scribes, Jesus always responded in the wisdom of the Scripture. This reveals that in order to become tough-minded you must give full attention to God's Word through meditation. Jesus could overcome every temptation that the devil, the Pharisees, the Sadducees and the Scribes posted at Him because He was full of the knowledge of God's Word and gave His attention to it.

In the same way, as a Christian, when you are full of the Word, it causes your mind to be strong enough to resist any temptation you're faced with. Paul the Apostle says in *Philippians 2:5 KJV* that *"Let this mind be in you, which was also in Christ Jesus..."* The question is what kind of mind did Jesus have? He had an undefeated mind that was not easily shaken or broken by sin or any temptation. This is the same mind that every Christian must operate in. Do not let sin and temptation ride over you, or guilt, shame and condemnation overshadow you. Be a tough-minded Christian! If you are struggling with lust, addictions, sexual impurities, or any kind of sin in your life or are being tempted in any way, what you need to do is to develop tough-mindedness. You do so by loading up yourself with the Word of God and yielding to the Voice of the Holy Spirit in your spirit.

When you study the Word of God, it unveils to you who you really are. So you no longer see yourself as one subject to sin, but rather as the righteousness of God in Christ Jesus. It gives you a clear picture that you have dominion over the works of the flesh [what appeals to your senses]. And the more you study the Word, the more conscious you become of the divine nature of God in you. This divine nature is superior to sin, sickness, wickedness, poverty, or any such thing.

Also, spending time to fellowship with God in prayer is another tool to help you maintain tough mindedness. In times of fellowship in prayer, the Holy Spirit makes you aware of the indwelling presence of God and releases Dunamis [Greek for might, force, strength or power] in you. The Bible says our bodies are the temple of God and the Spirit of God dwelleth in us. See 1 Corinthians 3:16 (KJV). Then, verse seventeen says, *"for the temple of God is holy, which temple ye are."* This simply means your body is special to God and is Godly influenced. Your body is God's, made by God and for God. Therefore, if you constantly remain conscious of the fact that *you* are holy and the presence of the Lord is in you, that builds your tough-mindedness and so no unclean thing or activity is able to take up residence in you.

When you face pressing situations in your life, do not allow yourself to feel weak or to say, "I can't handle it", for nothing can be above you as a child of God. The Scripture says that God will not let you face anything that you can't handle. See 1 Corinthians 10:13 (NIV). In other words, you are tough enough for anything! No challenge you face is above you! You are strong, agile and very courageous because you have a sound mind. Keep confessing that you have the mind of Christ and are tough enough to overcome every problem in your life. You are more than a conqueror and cannot be defeated.

I always say this to myself, "I'm tough enough for anything and not easily broken; therefore, I win all the time." Beloved, you can win all the time. I challenge you to be tough-minded, never allow your mind to become weak in doing what pleases God and always remain conscious of the fact that you are in right standing with God twenty-four-seven forever.

Supporting Scripture(s):

[1]SO, SINCE Christ suffered in the flesh for us, for you, arm yourselves with the same thought and purpose [patiently to suffer rather than

fail to please God]. For whoever has suffered in the flesh [having the mind of Christ] is done with [intentional] sin [has stopped pleasing himself and the world, and pleases God], [2] So that he can no longer spend the rest of his natural life living by [his] human appetites and desires, but [he lives] for what God wills.1 Peter 4:1-2 AMP

EXCERPT 11

Seated in Heavenly Places

✝

Hello! Many Christians pray for or desire a *lifting up* in their lives. They continuously ask God to lift them up in times of hardship or in times when they feel overpowered by the pressures of life. To this my question is, what are you still doing down there? Beloved, don't you know that the life of the Christian is already lifted up? You are not down any more; you have been lifted up! The Bible says *"And He raised us up together with Him and made us sit down together [giving us joint seating with Him] in the heavenly sphere [by virtue of our being] in Christ Jesus (the Messiah, the Anointed One)" Ephesians 2:6 AMP.*

In this verse, we see that God had <u>raised</u> us up together with Christ and made us sit in heavenly places with Him. Please pay close attention to the tense used in this verse. You'll notice the word 'raised' and 'made' is actually in the past tense. In other words, God is not making a promise here in this verse, He is making a statement of fact; a present hour reality. Therefore, you are not going to be raised up or lifted up; you are already lifted up with Christ and are seated in heavenly places with Him. Praise God! This is not for when we get to heaven, it is the now-reality of every believer!

I hear many people and sadly even Christians say "life is full of ups and downs". This is not true for the one who is born-again! You are now in Christ and as He is lifted up, you too are forever lifted up. No more ups and downs, just ups! Hallelujah! You may not feel up and lifted all the time, but being lifted up has nothing to do with your feelings. All you need to do is believe, accept and declare what God has said concerning you.

Dear Friend, these are not man's opinions put on paper for you to read; these are the truths in God's Word that I've come to discover. You see, religion says we are not qualified for this. It says we are not worthy enough, and that we can only sit with Him in heavenly places when we get to heaven. If you go back and read the scripture again, it didn't say "He *will make* us sit together in heavenly places when we get to heaven"; it said, He "…*hath made* us sit together". In other words, He's already done it and we are seated now. It is our now-experience.

Glory to God! Do you now see how raised and lifted you are? Why subject yourself to the mentality that says you'll experience ups and downs? Get rid of such thinking and start aligning your thoughts to what God has said about you, because that is your real identity.

Be conscious of the fact that you are seated in heavenly places with Christ. You don't have a low and downcast life; you are right up there with the Son of God Himself for He has called you to be a sharer and a partaker of His divine nature [glory]. See 2 Peter 1:2-4 (KJV). Praise God!

When you are conscious of this reality, you'll put a bounce to your steps, and walk with your head held high because now you know, you are seated with the King. So when you go out for the day's activities, you should go out with a sense of confidence knowing that you are divinely connected and a top class personnel. Hallelujah! I urge you by the Spirit of God to see yourself as God sees you: raised up and seated together with Christ.

Supporting Scripture(s):

[12]*Giving thanks unto the Father, which hath made us meet [qualified us] to be partakers of the inheritance of the saints in light:* [13]*Who hath delivered us from the power of darkness, and hath translated us into the kingdom of his dear Son. Colossians 1:12-13 KJV*

EXCERPT 12

Never lucky Ever blessed

✝

Hello! I've noticed that many people, including believers have become too fond of the phrases "wish me luck" or "good luck" or "lucky me". Many times, I hear a lot of Christians use words or phrases that are not really consistent to the life Christ has made available for us. The word *lucky* or *luck* refers to anything that happens by chance or unintended fortune. In other words, something that wasn't necessarily planned to happen; it just happened out of the blue. Also, the idea of luck gives the impression that it's temporal and not lasting. For example, if someone says he was lucky enough to find some money on the road, that doesn't mean that every day of his life now, he'll begin to pick money on the road. Therefore, what are the chances that he will have that kind of luck again and again? Luck doesn't happen all the time; it's just a onetime deal.

However, the Christian does not live by chance or by luck. The Christian is blessed! When you are blessed, it is not something that happens by chance or something that is unintended. When God blesses you, He doesn't do it by mistake. He had ordained every blessing you've received and will receive from the beginning of time. *Blessings are not mistaken; they are predestined* [Ephesians 1:3-5]. In fact, you can be sure that when God blesses you, it will last and will happen again and again as you desire and claim them. You as a child of God have been blessed for life! Glory to God! Let me make it totally clear; **the Christian is never lucky but ever blessed!**

The Scripture says, *"The blessing of the Lord—it makes [truly] rich, and He adds no sorrow with it [neither does toiling increase it]" Proverbs 10:22 AMP*. This means, as a child of God, you are too blessed to be stressed. The verse goes on to say that, this blessing adds no sorrow; neither does toiling increase in it. Oh I pray you can catch this in your spirit! Most people get paid depending on the amount of work or labor they do, but how would you like to get paid more than what you work for without any increase in labor? I bet that sounds like a great deal. This is what this scripture is talking about. It says when God blesses you; toiling [working] will not increase. This means you don't have to work hard to be a blessed man or woman. This is beyond luck! Luck has absolutely nothing to do with it, because this does not happen by chance. It happens by grace [unmerited favor]. God has preordained you for this!

As a child of God, you don't need luck when you are already blessed like that. Therefore, never wish to get lucky at anything or in any situation. In Christ, we have not only been blessed, but we have also been made [ordained] a blessing. You must understand that *the Blesser* [the Holy Ghost] lives in you and has made you a blessing. So you produce blessings now. You are the embodiment of all manner of blessings. As of now, instead of trying or wishing to get lucky, start proclaiming that you are a blessing. Refuse to be lucky and declare that you are blessed! Praise God! As you become more conscious of the fact that you are not only highly blessed, but you have been also ordained to be a blessing, you will begin to see the tangibility of God's manifold blessings unfold in your life. I charge you to always see yourself as someone who has been richly blessed and also been made a blessing.

Supporting Scripture(s):

[26]*And I will make them and the places round about My hill a blessing and I will cause the showers to come down in their season; there shall be showers of blessing [of good insured by God's favor].* [27]*And the tree of the field shall yield its fruit and the earth shall yield its increase; and [My people] shall be secure in their land, and they shall be confident and know (understand and realize) that I am the Lord, when I have broken the bars of their yoke and have delivered them out of the hand of those who made slaves of them.*[28]*And they shall no more be a prey to the nations, nor shall the beasts of the earth devour them, but they shall dwell safely and none shall make them afraid [in the day of the Messiah's reign]* [29]*And I will raise up for them a planting of crops for renown, and they shall be no more consumed with hunger in the land nor bear the reproach of the nations any longer. Ezekiel 34:26-29 AMP*

EXCERPT 13

Restoration

✝

Hello! Before I go further into this excerpt, I'd like to first of all touch on the concept of *restoration* and give you clarity on the subject. I have heard many interpret *restoration as taking back what the devil has stolen* or *going into the enemy's camp and recovering back all the devil has stolen from them*. But one day, while I was meditating on a scripture reference to this statement, I realized that these interpretations of restoration are not completely accurate with the Scripture. I asked myself two questions while meditating. What in the world will I be doing in the enemy's camp in the first place and why would I want anything back from the Devil? That scripture reference is...

Joel 2:25 KJV states, "And I will restore to you the years that the locust hath eaten, the cankerworm, and the caterpillar, and the palmerworm, my great army which I sent among you."

Notice in the beginning of the verse, it says "I", meaning God is the one to restore whatever the devil stole from you. The scripture did not say you will go into the enemy's camp and take anything from him. Trust me; you do not want anything the devil has to offer. Everything the devil has touched which was stolen from you is no longer good for you because it is now polluted and contaminated. So, when you ask the devil to return what he took from you, it is not the right prayer. Honestly, you will be asking for more trouble. God is the one and only true Restorer! If the devil has stolen anything from you, turn to God and ask Him to restore it. Don't ask the devil for anything!

In addition, when God says, *"I will restore..."* He is not talking about taking what was stolen from you by the devil and giving it back to you. He is simply saying there is more where the last one came from. Beloved, God has more than enough stored up for you; therefore ask no one but Him to restore those things in your life that you may have lost. You may have lost your job, money, home or anything else that was yours; God is more than able to restore it back to you. May be what you have lost is time itself, feeling you have wasted many years; I want you to know that God restores time as well. The Scripture said, "God will restore your wasted years, which are the years the locust has eaten." If I were you, I will begin to praise God because as you now know, God can give you back all that you have lost and even more. No longer should you feel sorry or down about whatever you have lost in the past. Instead, be exceedingly glad because you have a God who restores all things. Hallelujah!

Perhaps your case concerns your spiritual life; God can restore that too. I know of many Christians who have moved to a foreign region from their country of origin and are no longer as zealous and faithful in the things of God. Many say it's because the culture or life style is different. But in reality, it has nothing to do with the region you are in now. It doesn't really matter where you are, you can serve God faithfully if you set your heart to it. Your Christian life should not be determined by location and what's more, your life is supposed to be of greater influence to your location and what surrounds you, not the other way around. If you are reading this and you need God to restore your spiritual life to where it needs to be, God is more than willing to restore you back to Himself and put you back on the right path. Your dry bones can come alive again! (Ezekiel 37:1-14).

There is one very important piece you need to also look at when dealing with the subject of restoration:-*Don't be careless about what God restores back to you.* I have noticed many pray for God to restore them on Sunday, and the next Sunday they need another restoration on the same matter. Like a young child, every time you buy that child a new toy; they'll lose it and beg for another one. Don't be a spiritual baby by allowing the devil to consistently steal what God has blessed you. For one to be in need of restoration only means something has been taken away from him or her. When God restores you and gives you what you've lost, don't lose it again. Maintain that which you have received from God and don't allow the enemy to steal from you over and over.

How are you going to secure that which God has given you? By continually feeding on His Word, acting on the Word, speaking it over your life; and also learning to yield to the Holy Spirit. With these, you can't lose! I urge you to be conscious of these things that I've shared with you in this excerpt and you will see the restoration power of God at work in your life. Glory to God!

Supporting Scriptures(s):

Return to the stronghold [of security and prosperity], you prisoners of hope; even today do I declare that I will restore double your former prosperity to you. Zechariah 9:12 AMP

EXCERPT 14

How much can your Faith obtain?

Hello! How much can your faith obtain? This is a question that you should ask yourself every time you want something from God. Of course, in order to obtain much, you would also have to consider the size of the resource you are want to obtain from. Imagine there are two people who are going to carry water from the stream. One has a 5 gallon container and the other has a 10 gallon container. They each have to fill a 100 gallon container with the water from the stream. Which person do you think will fill up one hundred gallon container quicker? It is obvious that the one that has the 10 gallon container. Now the stream represents God [YOUR UNLIMITED RESOURCE], the 5 and 10 gallon containers are the different levels of faith, and the 100 gallons represents the lives of those two people. With greater faith you get quicker and better results. The Bible has made us to understand that we can't please God unless we have faith (Hebrews 11:6). To get more, our faith needs to grow to greater levels.

According to **Romans 12:3 KJV,** the Bible says everyone has been giving *the* measure of faith. Not *a* measure, but *the* measure. In other words, every Christian receives the exact same measure of faith on the day he or she is born again. No one starts with more faith than the other. However, it is the responsibility of each individual Christian to increase or grow *the* measure of faith that is given to him or her to a greater level. Sadly, many Christians still operate in the same level of faith they received when they just got saved. You need to know that there are greater levels of faith you can attain to so as to not settle at an infant stage. In fact, God expects every believer to grow his or her faith to the same level of faith He has. **Mark 11:22 (KJV)** declares, **"Have faith in God."** In the Greek, the correct rendering of the verse is, *"have the faith of God."* Our faith's destiny is to be at the level of God's faith. Does God exercise faith? Absolutely! There is not a single moment that

God will ever doubt Himself or what He can do. He is beyond confident, that all things are possible unto Him!

The level of faith you operate in, can determine your quality of life. If you have a middle class level of faith, you will live a middle class life; if you have a lower class level of faith, you will live a lower class life. But if you have an upper class level of faith, then an upper class life is what it will produce for you. Some Christians only have faith for small things and as a result, they live small lives. These are those who can barely get by in life; they only have enough for one day, one week, one month or a short period of time. This is because that's how much their faith can obtain for them. They can't seem to believe God for bigger things in life. When your faith is not big enough, you cannot get more than enough.

"But Pastor what about non-Christians who are very wealthy and living big, do they have more faith than Christians?"

One thing you must understand is that there are certain laws or principles in the Bible that is universal—anyone can get the benefits of it if they apply these principles. This is what the Bible means when it says, *"...for he maketh his sun to rise on the evil and on the good, and sendeth rain on the just and on the unjust" (Matthew 5:45 KJV).* The truth is many unbelievers apply these principles sometimes even without knowing and it yields results for them. For example, the *law of gravity* is a law that states that things that go up tend to fall back downwards. Now, if someone without the knowledge of this law, throws up an object, again even without the knowledge of the downward pull of gravity, will the object still respect the law of gravity? Emphatically yes! This is the same with the law or principle of faith. Many unbelievers are wealthy; because they have applied God's principles for wealth without even know it.

There many Christians around the world and especially in third world countries who are suffering from extreme poverty because they have not yet applied God's principles in their live in the area of wealth. One can have great faith in their health and very little faith in their finances and vice versa. But God wants you to operate in greater faith in every area of your life so you can live the higher life that He wants you to live. Have great faith in all areas! So grow in faith not in the spiritual, but also in the physical, material, financial, educational and even emotional aspects. Don't have a successful career and have a damaged marriage or have a lot of money and you are not spiritually saved, that is, to be born-again. God's best for you is that you prosper in all areas. See 3 John 1:2 KJV.

Also, your faith must get big enough to look beyond what your natural eyes can see. As a child of God, you've got to learn to look beyond and carry more than what your optical eyes can see. See through the eyes of your spirit. When God said to Abraham to look northward, southward, westward, eastward and as far as his eyes could see that all he can see will be his inheritance (See Genesis 13:14-17 KJV). If Abraham looked with his natural born eyes; naturally and geographically, he would only see about a few miles in each direction. But I believe that Abraham looked through the eyes of his spirit and saw the world at large and that was exactly what God gave to him for an inheritance. His faith was big enough to see beyond his natural family. Abraham saw nations and kingdoms, from every tribe and every tongue although he did not have a child of his own at the time. Wow, that's big faith! And the Scripture says God willed the whole world to Abraham.

Let me ask you dear friend, how big is your faith? How much can your faith carry from God [the stream] for you? Don't go to the stream [God] with small gallons [faith]. If you do, you won't be able to carry much with it and it will take you a longer time to fill up your life with all the good things you so desire. Therefore, improve and develop on your faith. Don't let it remain small or as the same measure you had when you got born again. Why not believe God for more than you can see and watch your life gush out the miraculous.

Begin to see God change that child you think will never make it in life. See God changing the situation of that marriage that you feel divorce is the end result. See Him restoring your home, prospering you, giving you good children, blessing you with a wonderful wife or husband, and doing bigger things for you. No matter how big or impossible you think it may be, believe God for it. See God doing the impossible! If you are going to believe God for anything, you might as well believe Him for something big. God loves challenges; He never shies away from them, however, in reality, nothing is a challenge to Him because He is super-able! Refuse to be small in life. Don't settle for less, go for the best!

You may say "well I don't think I deserve anything big from God". First of all, you must understand that as a Christian there is a difference between when you were not born-again and now that you are born-again. The sacrifice of Jesus on the cross was not for nothing. It qualifies anyone who is born-again for anything; therefore, as a child of God, you qualify for God's best! You are no longer undeserving; you have been qualified! The

Word says in *Colossians 1:12 NIV* *"giving thanks to the Father, who has qualified you to share in the inheritance of the saints in the kingdom of light."* So don't feel undeserving, give thanks! He has qualified you, He is not going to or will do it later; He's already done it! Hallelujah! You deserve whatever you ask in faith from the Lord. The blood of Jesus Christ has paid it ALL. We are now freely enjoying what Christ has paid for. And for you not to enjoy all the blessings Christ paid for and just wanting small portions of these blessings, is like wasting all He did for you. Who wants to buy something and not enjoy the full benefits of what he or she bought. It would be considered to be a waste if not fully enjoyed. Beloved, all you desire from God has already been paid for. So ask freely and enjoy all the benefits you have in Christ. I challenge you by the power of God to take advantage of the already paid blessings of Christ and develop your faith to greater levels so you can obtain greater things from the stream [God]. Hallelujah!

Supporting Scripture(s):

[8] *[Urged on] by faith Abraham, when he was called, obeyed and went forth to a place which he was destined to receive as an inheritance; and he went, although he did not know or trouble his mind about where he was to go.* [9] *[Prompted] by faith he dwelt as a temporary resident in the*

land which was designated in the promise [of God, though he was like a stranger] in a strange country, living in tents with Isaac and Jacob, fellow heirs with him of the same promise. [10] For he was [waiting expectantly and confidently] looking forward to the city which has fixed and firm foundations, whose Architect and Builder is God.

Hebrews 11:8-10 AMP

Who through faith subdued kingdoms, wrought righteousness, obtained promises, stopped the mouths of lions. Hebrews 11:33 KJV

EXCERPT 15

How to grow your faith

✝

Hello! Remember in the previous excerpt, I shared with you a scripture on *the* measure of faith. I would like us to look into that scripture again. *"For by the grace given me I say to every one of you: Do not think of yourself more highly than you ought, but rather think of yourself with sober judgment, <u>in accordance with the measure of faith God has given you"</u> Romans 12:3 NIV.* As I explained in the last excerpt, God gives everyone at the point of salvation or when they get born again *the measure* of faith, not *a measure*. This means we all get the same measure [amount] of faith at salvation. No one gets more than the other. As a matter of fact, Jesus

Christ started with the same level too when He was on earth and as you would know, He grew His faith to greater levels.

To grow in faith, it is the responsibility of the Christian. You've got to increase from the initial level you started with to greater dimensions. The initial portion you receive at salvation is not enough to sustain you in your Christian walk. Therefore, growing in faith is imperative for every Christian. Don't let your faith remain idle. Your spiritual growth is dependent on your faith growth. If you are not growing your faith, you will find difficulties fulfilling the plan of God for your life and experiencing the manifestation of the fullness of God. So, how do you grow your faith? There are some few keys that I have learned on how to grow my faith that I'd like to share with you. They are as follows…

1. *The Bible says in Romans 10:17 KJV, "So then faith cometh by hearing, and hearing by the word of God." In other words, the Word of God is what produces faith. No Word, no faith. This is beautiful! The Word of God is the source of faith. We don't have to go far to get it or pay to have it, we can get it from His Word. Halleluiah! So spend time listening to and studying God's Word every day. Let everyday be an opportunity to add to the present level of faith you have.*

2.   Now, just having a Bible or just reading the Bible doesn't necessarily increase one's faith. What do you do? You begin by meditating [contemplating, visualizing and memorizing] on the Word as you read or hear it. Next, you act on the Word you've read or heard. Acting on God's Word means practicing or doing it says. For faith to grow, it requires corresponding action. James 1:22 says we should "...be doers of the word, not hearers only..." If your faith will grow to greater levels, you must continue doing the Word. When you do what the Word says, it produces results and that gives you more faith for next time so you can believe for more and better things.

3.   Another thing you should always do as a child of God is to speak forth God's Word. You've got to say it out! You may say "I don't need to speak it out, but as long as I believe it in my heart that's what counts." Please do not be deceived, what you believe you speak. In fact, no one knows if you truly believe in something until you have spoken about it. I've found out each time I constantly speak God's Word over my life, I feel so energized and ready to take on the world. Why? Because it increase my faith and I am stirred up on the inside. Speaking God's Word makes you even more assured of what the Word talks about. As you speak it forth, that Word settles in your spirit, at this time, no one can tell you otherwise. You believe, and are sure and certain about it. Glory to God!

4. *The scripture says in Galatians 5:6, "...but faith which worketh by love." The Amplified version says, "...but only faith activated and energized and expressed and working through love." Faith works directly proportional to Love. Without Love you can't walk in faith; therefore, to grow in faith, you must grow in Love. The Bible says Jesus had compassion on the sick and those who came to Him for their healing. That's Love! No wonder He walked in such a high level of faith. When you love more, you make room for faith to be expressed in greater capacity.*

5. *Praying in other tongues will also enhance or build up your faith. Jude vs. 20 says, "...building up yourself, on your most holy faith, praying in the Holy Ghost. Wow! That means when you pray in other tongues, you are increasing your faith and not only increasing it, but increasing it from its current maximum level to a new maximum. When you pray in other tongues, your faith rises to its topmost level and it continues from there. This is so awesome!*

Your faith must constantly develop or grow in order for you to take on greater challenges in life and experience greater success. Don't let it stay on the same level for too long. Increase your faith. The higher level of faith you operate in, the better your life will become. I challenge you to improve and develop your faith from its present level.

Supporting Scripture(s):

We ought and indeed are obligated [as those in debt] to give thanks always to God for you, brethren, as is fitting, <u>because your faith is growing exceedingly and the love of every one of you each toward the others is increasing and abounds.</u> 2 Thessalonians 1:3 AMP

EXCERPT 16

What do you see?

✟

Hello! There are many Christians who are not satisfied with the quality of life they have. If you were to ask some Christians you may know, I would say a good number of them would say they are not enjoying their life. Nowadays when you ask someone "how are you doing?" they'll make statements like, "I'm managing" or "I'm hanging in there" or even worse "I'm struggling". This is how many Christians see themselves living. They never see themselves as making any progress in life.

Also, there are those who all they talk about is what they used to be. You hear them say, "I used to be a strong Christian, I used to give, I used to be very smart or I used to live a good life."

My question for you is how do you see yourself now and in the future? Can you see yourself doing the things you used to do and even do them better than you did before? What you are able to see today, will determine what manner of life you will have tomorrow.

Behold, I give unto you power to tread on serpents and scorpions, and over all the power of the enemy: and nothing shall by any means hurt you.
Luke 10:19 KJV

In the above scripture, the Bible says, *Behold*, another word for it is *"see"*, and as I'd like to put it, *"Can't you see?"* I [Jesus] give unto to you power to tread [trample, make to nothing by stepping] upon serpents [the devil and demonic spirits] and scorpions [death and evil] and over all the power of the enemy [sickness, disease, poverty, wickedness, sin, temptation, guilt, shame, condemnation]: and nothing shall by any means hurt you. Praise the Lord! So I ask again, what do you see? Do you see yourself overcoming the circumstances you are facing or do see yourself being defeated?

The Bible says in *1 Samuel 17:45-46 KJV:*

" ⁴⁵Then said David to the Philistine, Thou comest to me with a sword, and with a spear, and with a shield: but I come to thee in the name of the LORD of hosts, the God of the armies of Israel, whom thou hast defied. ⁴⁶This day will the LORD deliver thee into mine hand; and I will smite thee, and take thine head from thee; and I will give the carcasses of the host of the Philistines this day unto the fowls of the air, and to the wild beasts of the earth; that all the earth may know that there is a God in Israel."

As you continue to read this chapter, you find out that, what David said he was going to do, was exactly what he did. He gave specific and vivid description as to how this giant, Goliath, was going to die. David, the young lad, confronted Goliath and told him how he was going to die before he ever killed him. Wow, David had to have seen something the army of Israel was not able to see.

I believe he saw the overcoming power of God at work in his life. Also, because of what God used David to do in the past-defeating the bear and the lion in the field of his flock, he was able to see himself taking down the giant too. Can you see this same power available and at work in your life or do you see weakness, struggles, hurt, shame, pain, poverty, sin, and all other negative things taking charge of your life? What do you see?

I want you to understand that God gave us an imagination to visualize who we are in Christ and what we can do for Him. Don't use that imagination the wrong way. The Scripture says, *"...Casting down imaginations, and every high thing that exalteth itself against the knowledge of God, and bringing into captivity every thought to the obedience of Christ..." 2 Corinthians 10:5 KJV.* Therefore, don't visualize negative things or have negative thoughts about your life. When they try to come up, cast them down!

Don't believe everything you see with your natural eyes either. Not everything you see is real. Those problems you have are just there to shake you and cause you to fear. But refuse to see your problems and set your attention to their solutions. Your problems are unreal! Act as though they are not there and refuse to recognize their presence or their effects. This is not being delusional; rather, it is taking sides with the Word. Whatever the Word of God has said concerning you; it becomes your reality and everything that is contrary to it becomes a lie. Instead of seeing sickness, see and speak health, instead of seeing failure, see and speak success. Open your eyes and begin to see blessings, strength, success, favor, love, peace, joy, wealth, good health, and victory, even if it doesn't look like it in the natural. Keep seeing what you want and what God has said concerning your situation and you will have exactly what you are able to see. You can get what you want from God and live the kind of life you desire, if you can only see it. I urge you to see yourself progressing and not digressing.

Supporting Scripture(s):

Looking away [from all that will distract] to Jesus, Who is the Leader and the Source of our faith [giving the first incentive for our belief] and is also the Finisher [bringing it to maturity and perfection]. He, for the joy [of obtaining the prize] that was set before Him, endured the cross, despising and ignoring the shame, and is now seated at the right hand of the throne of God. Hebrews 12:2 AMP

EXCERPT 17

Praying and Encouraging the Strong

✝

Hello! There are people who God has put at the war front; those who are spiritually stronger than others, so-to-speak, those who may be known to be more committed to the work of the kingdom, and those who God has given higher callings. They may be your pastor, bishop, leaders in church, parents, youth leader, prayer leader, or cell leader in the area you live. These are people we look up to; we see them as our role models. For example, if you had a problem that you cannot handle and need spiritual guidance, these are the people you would go to for assistance. While it is necessary that the weak in faith should often be interceded for and encouraged, it is also very vital that we give the same efforts and attention in praying and encouraging those we know to be stronger in faith.

In the book of *Ephesians 6:18-19 KJV*, the scripture says, "...*[18]Praying always with all prayer and supplication in the Spirit, and watching thereunto with all perseverance and supplication for all saints; [19]And for me, that utterance may be given unto me, that I may open my mouth boldly, to make known the mystery of the gospel...*" In this verse, Paul the Apostle requested for the Church at Ephesus to pray for him. You must understand that Paul was their spiritual leader; the one who the Christians at Ephesus looked up to as a person of influence and someone who was spiritually stronger or more mature. Yet, he requested for their prayer. This is to show us that no one is above prayer or encouragement and Paul understood that. Even though he was spiritually stronger, he still needed the prayer of those who were under him. A lot of believers fail to lift up their spiritual leaders in prayer because they feel those who spiritually mature people are strong enough to pray and encourage themselves and don't need their prayer. Therefore, instead of wasting their time praying for someone who is already strong, they'll rather use that time to pray for themselves or someone they believe is weak in faith.

I find it really sad, when many Christians will speak ill of ministers who may have been caught in the middle of a scandal. The Bible never suggests that we join the world to ridicule those in our own household of faith even if they may be at fault. But you see many believers are the first speak against ministers, showing no respect for their office. As a Christian you should be aware that those God has given you as spiritual leaders, are representatives Him [God Himself]. So if you speak ill about a minister, you are speaking ill against God as well. Again, irrespective of what they have done or what you think they are doing wrong, it will be wise not to speak evil of any man or woman of God. This is very important. This is why God was so offended at Miriam for venturing to speak against her brother Moses, and was cursed with leprosy. See Numbers 12. I will expound more on this in an upcoming volume. However, be wise enough to lift up spiritual leaders instead of partaking with those who talk down on them. This is the character of a spirit-filled believer. Let your love and passion for those in place of leadership grow. Give them your best support. They will greatly appreciate it!

I've also realized that many times we tend to bless or give only to those who we think don't have. For instance, some believers find it difficult to bless a rich person because he already has enough. They would rather bless someone who doesn't have much and will benefit more from what they give. This kind of mentality is not completely in line with God's Word. The Bible does not tell us or suggest that a stronger Christian doesn't need the prayer or blessings because they are stronger. Everyone, at every level deserves to be blessed, prayed for and encouraged.

Remember that the more we grow in Christ, the greater the level of oppositions we encounter; in other words, *Greater levels Greater devils*. As a Christian, you should learn to always pray for your pastors, leaders, teachers, parents, mentors or those you know to be stronger and encourage them too. Even if you can't think of anything to pray or encourage them about, which I'm sure will rarely be the case, at least pray and encourage them to stay strong or get stronger; for if they don't stay strong, you won't have them to look up to. Keep this in mind that even the *strong* needs strength. As you spend time praying and encouraging those who are weak, keep in mind that those who are *strong* also need your prayer and support.

Supporting Scripture(s):

[2]*Continue in prayer, and watch in the same with thanksgiving;*
[3]*Withal* **praying also for us***, that God would open unto us a door of*

utterance, to speak the mystery of Christ, for which I am also in bonds: ⁴*That I may make it manifest, as I ought to speak.*

Colossians 4:2-4 KJV

1*I urge, then, first of all, that requests, prayers, intercession and thanksgiving be made for everyone—* **2***for kings and all those in authority, that we may live peaceful and quiet lives in all godliness and holiness.* **3***This is good, and pleases God our Savior,* **4***who wants all men to be saved and to come to the knowledge of the truth. 1 Timothy 2:1-4 NIV*

EXCERPT 18

Exploring God's Word

‡

Hello! What is your purpose for studying God's Word and do you have a cause [reason] for doing so? Many Believers read or study their Bible as a religious duty or just as one of the things in a daily schedule they have to do. They read the Bible as if it were some kind of novel or textbook. Some Christians have only managed to read a few books in the Bible. The only books they've majored on of all are Psalm and Proverbs. If you were to ask them what they've read from them, they will tell you something like, "I got something out of it but I forgot what it was" or "well let me look at it again and tell you". A common one is, "I didn't really get what I was reading so I stopped because I was getting bored". Whatever they read from the Bible doesn't mean anything to them because they are trying to mark it off their checklist as one of the things to do for the day.

Make no mistake that as long as you read the Bible that way you can't be effective in your Christian walk. I also find it sad that even though there are many Christians who read the Bible like this; there are still so many who hardly ever pick up their Bible to read at all. They've got no relationship whatsoever with the Bible, and the truth is they have no interest in it. This is a growing problem in the church today.

How can one expect to live beyond the pressures of life when he keeps the Word so far away from him? It wouldn't make sense to pray for God to deliver you from all kinds of trouble when so much distance is kept from His Word. Remember God's Word is salient for good success in life; therefore, abstaining from His Word has a negative impact on us. When God wants to do something great or change something in your life, He sends His Word to do it. The Bible says, *"He sent his word, and healed them, and delivered them from their destructions." Psalm 107:20 KJV.* The Word of God is what the believer needs to excel in life.

Dear friend, why in the world should you read the Bible? You must have a purpose or a reason for reading the Bible; otherwise it won't mean anything to you or have any effect in your life. Your purpose must be beyond simply reading it, beyond cramming it as a memory verse and beyond just reading to fulfill a religious duty. So, why should anyone read the Bible? Well, I'll tell you.

In today's world, things happen every day that can attempt to raise troubled questions in our minds. To many people, it seems today we have a lot more questions than answers. Questions like, "if God really exists then why do people suffer every day?" or "why is there so much evil in the world?" When someone doesn't have the accurate information of what the Word says about particular issues, these kinds of questions will rise up in the mind. As you read the Bible consistently, you will realize that your doubts are being dissolved and your questions about life are being answered.

Jesus said to His Father in *John 17:17 KJV,* "*...thy word is truth...*" Truth means *reality.* God's Word [the Bible] is reality; it is what the Christian knows to be reality. In other words, the Bible is the reference point of everything. If you need to know the truth about something, you can find it in the Bible. This is the reason the Bible was given to us because God knew that we are going to have questions about the world we live in and about our lives. God is the master planner. Before you ever had a problem, He had first thought of the solution. That solution is His Word!

The Bible is like a land filled with hidden treasures. You have to search it properly to find these treasures. As a Christian, your responsibility is to explore God's Word to discover the hidden treasures in it. There are things in the Bible you won't discover by just speed-reading or reading it for only ten minutes a day. You would need to spend time studying to dig out what you need. For example, I've heard many say the reason Jesus Christ came was to die for our sins. But when you study and explore the Bible in its entirety, you'll discover that the reason Jesus Christ came was not to die for our sins. Yes, He did that, but that's not why He came. He had to die for sins in order to do what He came to do. *John 10:10 (KJV)* says, *"the thief cometh not, but for to steal, to kill and to destroy..."* Now here is what Jesus said He came to do, *"...but I am come, that they might have life and have it more abundantly [Greek: to the full].* If you don't spend time with the Word, you'll always go with what you heard someone said about the Bible or assumptions you made when you were young and never really finding out the truth for yourself. The Word of God tells you who you really are, not what you think you are or what people say you are, but what God says you are. It lets you know all that has been made available to you in Christ. These realities have to be located by spending quality time to dig the

Word. God's plan for your life is hidden in His Word and you must take time to find it out.

A lot of people are not making progress in life because they don't know how to. But with the Word of God, you can discover how to make progress everyday of your life. As a child of God, you cannot succeed without the Word. Success comes from the Word. Success does not come by years of experience or your qualifications, that's the way of the World. For a believer, your success is from the Word. See Joshua 1:8 (KJV). May be you never went to school to get a degree, you are not limited. The Word of God super-able to propel you to success. Even if you didn't come from a well-to-do or rich background or maybe you didn't have a parent to guide you in life, with the Word, your success is still possible. The Word can be for you what your parents could not! It can be your rich background. You cannot be at a disadvantage with the Word! These are the realities that are in the Word of God and if you can only spend time with it, it will change your life and the world around you.

Many years ago, when I was growing up as a young believer, I used to live by other people's interpretation of the Word and never studied it for myself. I later found out that I was being steered into many misconceptions and got the wrong understanding of the Bible. Many Christians still live this way. They are comfortable and satisfied with whatever they learn on Sundays, at bible study or with what their pastor teach them. They never verify it on their own for themselves to see if what they learned is accurate and *complete*. I used the word *"complete"* because, you may learn the truth, but is that the *whole* truth? Many times you can hear a half-truth, and you think it's the whole truth, but it's really not. For example, I grew up believing in healing and still do. Now healing is a truth when it comes to the heath of a Christian, but that's not the whole truth. Healing is in your body is possible, but I also came to discover something further than healing. It's called divine health; where you are never in need of a healing because you don't get sick. You see, revelation is progressive. In this domain of divine health: where you know no sickness or infirmity because you have the life and nature of God in you that is immune to any sickness. Third John 1:2 says God wants us to *be in health*. Not get sick and then get healed, He says, *be in health*. Meaning God wants us to stay healthy! It takes exploring to find higher revelations in the Word to live by. Your pastor may not tell you, not because he doesn't want to, but the truth is, he may not even know himself. Therefore, it's your responsibility to verify what your pastor teaches you and also grow in revelation of what you learn. This you have to find out for yourself. Regard the teachings of your pastors or your leaders, but also get a confirmation on what he or she says by exploring the Word for your own self-knowledge. It will have greater impact in your life if you know the truth for yourself rather than just following it blindly.

2 Timothy 2:15 KJV says, *"Study to show thyself approved unto God, a workman that needeth not to be ashamed, rightly dividing the word of Truth."* This is so powerful! It says study to show yourself approved. This doesn't mean you study God's Word to brag that you know it. It means to study it until you are approved by it [changed by it, transformed by it, invigorated by it, catalyzed by it] and as the Word approves you, then you can rightly divide [teach, explain, preach] it to others. If the Word has had an effect in your life, it will of necessity have an effect in the lives of those you tell it to. When it has modified and caused a fundamental change in your life, then you will be compelled to tell everyone about it and you'll notice the tangible results that will follow.

Be sure you have complete understanding of what the Word is talking about. This is how you can develop in every area of your life. The more you increase in the knowledge of the God's Word, the simpler life becomes for you. Your effectiveness in life is dependent on your Bible knowledge and the accuracy of the understanding of that knowledge. Be an explorer of God's Word—a Word specialist. Let people know you as a Word Doctor. I challenge you to explore God's Word and spend time in it, for in it, lays the power to change you, your circumstances and those you tell it to.

Supporting Scripture(s):

[16]*All scripture is given by inspiration of God, and is profitable for doctrine, for reproof, for correction, for instruction in righteousness:* [17]*That the man of God may be perfect, thoroughly furnished unto all good works.*

2 Timothy 3:16-17KJV

EXCERPT 19

Understanding God's Word

✝

Hello! Many times I've heard people say the Bible is contradictory and when they read the Bible it doesn't make sense to them. Some say they get bored or fall asleep as soon as they pick up their Bibles to read. I suggest that this could be the result of a lack of the understanding of the God's Word. The Bible says in *Proverbs 4:7 KJV, "Wisdom is the principal thing; therefore get wisdom: and with all thy getting get understanding."* It says as you take hold of God's wisdom [His Word]; with all the wisdom you get, get understanding also. Understanding means to comprehend, discern, perceive and to grasp.

For the Word of God to fully manifest in you and be in constant operation in you, you must be able to comprehend it. No matter how many chapters you read from the Bible, it will not make any difference in your life if you do not have accurate understanding of it.

Without accurate understanding of God's Word, you can believe the wrong thing and suffer things that you ought not to. The enemy is tormenting many people because they don't have adequate understanding of God's Word. For example, some people, when they are sick, they think that God is punishing them for their sins. God doesn't punish you with sickness because you sinned. In fact, God doesn't ever punish you for sinning.

"But Pastor Glovis doesn't the Bible say that the wages of sin is death?"

Yes it does, the wages of sin is death. But the good news is that death did take place already. Jesus died to pay the full price for every sin and took upon Himself all consequences or punish for sins so that those who believe in Him and His finished work won't have to be punished for their sins. Jesus was punished for your sins, so God cannot punish you again for them. He will be unjust to punish Jesus and you for the same sins. Therefore, because Christ was punished, you are free from the penalty of your sins. You have been discharge and acquitted [Justified]! See

Romans 5:1. What I'm saying is this: without having accurate understanding of God's Word, you can continue believing the wrong thing until it finally kills you.

The Scripture says Jesus said to His disciples, *"But the Comforter (Counselor, Helper, Intercessor, Advocate, Strengthener, Standby), the Holy Spirit, Whom the Father will send in my name [in my place, to represent me and act on my behalf], He will teach you all things. And He will cause you to recall (will remind you of, bring to your remembrance) everything I have told you" John 14:26 AMP.* This verse says the Holy Spirit is the one to bring all things to your remembrance. To bring to remembrance also means to enlighten the eyes of your understanding. To receive accurate understanding of God's Word is to allow the Holy Spirit to teach you the Word and grant you clarity into what it talks about.

Early in Excerpt three, we talked about meditation. Meditating is another way to help you understand God's Word. When you meditate on the Word, you give time for the Holy Spirit to bring about clarity and insight on what you are reading. Meditation is spiritual digestion. It will help you absorb the information properly and process it, so it soaks your consciousness. At this time, everything becomes clear to you and you have a more accurate understanding of what you are reading.

You can <u>also</u> refer to different translations of the Bible. Some translations explain things in greater details than others. Take advantage of the cross references in your Bible and go through a Bible concordance to find similar scriptures that will help you understand what you're reading better. I highly recommend that you take the extra step to look into the Greek and Hebrew meanings of certain words or expressions to understand what the Bible is talking about in specific places. But know this, you must always be guided by the Holy Spirit in you and rely on Him to give you the accurate truth of God's Word. I encourage you dear friend to not only seek the knowledge of the Word but a precise understanding thereof.

Supporting Scripture(s):

17That the God of our Lord Jesus Christ, the Father of glory, may give unto you the spirit of wisdom and revelation in the knowledge of him: 18The eyes of your understanding being enlightened; that ye may know what is the hope of his calling, and what the riches of the glory of his inheritance in the saints, 19And what is the exceeding greatness of his power to us-ward who believe, according to the working of his mighty power.

Ephesians 1:17-19 KJV

EXCERPT 20

Cooperating with the Holy Spirit

✝

Hello! One of the biggest issues believers struggle with today is the issue of cooperating with the Holy Spirit. Cooperating with the Holy Spirit is needed if you are going to function effectively in your Christian life. Those who do not relate well with the Holy Spirit always have something they are struggling with; something that's holding them back from moving forward into higher levels in the things of God. There are a lot of Christians having difficulties letting go of some kind of sin, bad habit, bad attitude, or negativity. These are those who are perpetually in the same place with no improvements. I believe the main reason for such inactiveness in a Christian is that they have not yet yielded completely to the Holy Spirit. If you are ever going to be successful in your walk with Christ, the Holy Spirit is the person you need to cooperate with to make that happen. Are you satisfied with your Christian walk at this point or do you think you can do better? Friend, the Holy Spirit is earnestly waiting for you to cooperate with Him.

But first and foremost, who is the Holy Spirit and what did He come to do? How can you cooperate with someone you don't know? It is sad to know that many Christians do not know who the Holy Spirit is. What I have noticed is that many Christians believe the Holy Spirit is some type of force or power. Others think He is a tongue, a white dove (as illustrated in art), or as a wind. I'd like to formally introduce to you who the Holy Spirit really is. The Holy Spirit has always been, is and will always be a *person*. Why is He a person? Well, because you can have a relationship with Him. He is not a force or power, although He gives power to do God's will [which is God's Word]; He is not a tongue, although He gives the utterance to speak in other tongues; and He is definitely not a dove, although He descended in the **manner** [behavior or style] of a dove. He is God the Holy Spirit; the third person of the God-head-*the Trinity*.

Now that you know who the Holy Spirit is, let's get back to cooperating with the Holy Spirit. When you become born-again and receive the infilling of the Holy Spirit, He comes to live in your spirit. He is the one that makes you a Christian and without Him Christ cannot be in you. Therefore, as a Christian, it is of utmost importance for you to know why He came to live in you; otherwise, your Christian walk will not mean anything to you. In the book of *John 14:16-17 KJV*, Jesus said to His disciples,

"16And I will pray the Father and he shall give you another Comforter that he may abide with you forever. 17Even the Spirit of truth; whom the world cannot receive, because it seeth him not, neither knoweth him: but ye know him; for he dwelleth with you, and shall be in you."

The word *Comforter* from the Greek translation is *Parakletos*, which also means *Counselor, Helper, Intercessor, Advocate, Strengthener, and Standby*. The Holy Spirit is all these things to the Christian, and more. So it will be impossible to be a success in your Christian life without you cooperating with Him.

We need to understand that as much as the Holy Spirit desires to be a counselor, helper, intercessor, advocate, strengthener and a standby to us, we must be completely willing to cooperate with Him at all times. I find it amazing how many of us want help from the Holy Spirit but do not want to take heed to His instructions. If a billionaire wanted to help you become rich, wouldn't you listen to him or her and do what he or she tells you? I'm sure you will. But the Holy Spirit can do exceedingly better than what anybody can do for you.

His instructions have the ability to make you a success in every domain of life. You'll be amazed at what He can achieve in your life when you cooperate with Him. He loves you and He's there to help. I'll share more on the Five-P's [person, personality, promise, purpose and power] of the Holy Spirit in my upcoming book called *Allos Parakletos*. I encourage you to train yourself to cooperate with the Holy Spirit everyday of your life and by so doing you will experience success in greater dimensions.

Supporting Scripture(s):

But the Comforter (Counselor, Helper, Intercessor, Advocate, Strengthener, Standby), the Holy Spirit, Whom the Father will send in my name [in my place, to represent me and act on my behalf], He will teach you all things. And He will cause you to recall (will remind you of, bring to your remembrance) everything I have told you. John 14:26 AMP

EXCERPT 21

The Power of Grace

✝

Hello! In *Romans 5:20 AMP*, the Bible says, *"...But where sin increased and abounded, grace has surpassed it and increased the more and super-abounded..."* Many times we have let a sin or weakness put us in place we are not supposed to be. A lot Christians go through the motions of constantly coming to God to ask for His forgiveness for a particular sin they just can seem to overcome. And as a result, they find themselves carrying the weight of shame, guilt and condemnation because they are constantly struggling with a certain sin. Beloved, the scripture we just read said *"where sin increased and abound, [God's] grace has surpassed it and increased the more and super-abounded."* This means that no matter how strong you think that particular sin is, when you become conscious of the ever-increasing grace of God in your life, sin's power loses stability in your life.

One thing I've discovered about God's grace is that it doesn't only free you from sin; it also keeps you from it. There are many Christians who believe that God's grace is only available for each time they sin. For example, someone will continue to commit sin because he thinks the grace of God is always there, so he becomes comfortable in that sin because he has grace. Beloved, grace is not an excuse to sin. Remember Paul said in *Romans 6:1 KJV* that, *"...shall we continue in sin, that grace may abound?"* Let me rephrase the question like this: *Can you continue in sin, when grace has abounded?* This is a very thought-provoking question. I believe Apostle Paul was trying to suggest that it was not possible for a Christian who has received a surpassing, increasing and super-abounding grace in his or her life to continue in sin. I say this because of what he said in the next verse. *"God Forbid. How shall we that are dead to sin, live any longer therein?"* He is **not** saying that *we are going to die to sin*; He says **we are dead to sin**. That statement is not a conditional statement or a promise. It is a statement of fact; a present-our-reality. When you got born again, you died to sin. The reason many Christians still struggle with sin is because they think they are still trying to die to it. You must understand that for a Christian to keep living a sinful life defeats the purpose of Christ's death. Jesus Christ dealt with the issue of sin once and for all. That's why in the same book of *Romans 6:14 KJV* it says, *"For sin shall not have dominion over you: for ye are not under the law, but under grace."* In other words, the one who is under the influence of grace cannot be subjected to sin or a sinful life-style. Hallelujah! This is reality! The reason a lot of Christians keep sinning is because they are still under the influence of the law (trying to please God by works or self-efforts). As far as God is concern, the Christian is God's beloved in whom He is well pleased. The Christian is not trying to please God by not sinning; he is already pleasing to the Father, because he has been brought into right standing [made righteous] with Him through the Blood of Jesus Christ. See Romans 5:1. Knowing this reality is what empowers you for righteous living.

Dear Friend, you are not subject to sin; you are far above it because you have the nature of God working in you now. And that nature is superior to sin or sinning. Can you believe, accept, confess and walk in this truth? As a born again child of God, you must know that you are now an absolutely new man. Not an improved version of your old man or a better kind of the same.

No! You are a perfectly New Creation in Christ and this new man is dead to sin and fully alive to the God-life. Now you talk, respond, operate and live like God. Praise God!

Don't let the enemy tell you that you lack the ability to come out of that sin or weakness, for God's grace is strong, powerful, and mightily at work in you. Overcoming struggles with sin and weakness in your life is achieved when you acknowledge that His grace has surpassed your sins and weaknesses and is super-abounding in you. For this cause, every Christian should walk in excellence and overcome sin all the time! Again I tell you, you are not subject to sin my dear friend; you are totally above it! I challenge you to refuse to acknowledge the controlling power of sin in your life and be awakened to the dominating power of grace mightily at work in you! Praise God!

Supporting Scripture(s):

[1]There is therefore now no condemnation to them which are in Christ Jesus; who walk not after the flesh but after the Spirit. [2]For the law of the Spirit of life [Grace] in Christ Jesus hath made me free from the law of sin and death. Romans 8:1-2 KJV

EXCERPT 22

You are the Head and not the Tail

✝

Hello! *"And the LORD shall make thee the head, and not the tail; and thou shalt be above only, and thou shalt not be beneath; if that thou hearken unto the commandments of the LORD thy God, which I command thee this day, to observe and to do them:" Deuteronomy 28:13 KJV.* There are many Christians today who haven't really experienced what it means to be the head and live above only. They've taken the words *"living above only and not beneath"* as some type of a religious cliché. One thing you must come to a conclusion on as a child of God is, believing that God's Word is Truth-*reality* and that whatever He says about you is your reality. Otherwise, you will doubt what God has said concerning you instead of being a living prove of what He has said. The Bible says that *"God is not man that He should lie" Numbers 23:19 (KJV)*.

The passage you just read from the beginning says that God shall or will make you the head and not the tail, above only and not beneath is now a present-hour-reality to those who are in Christ Jesus. When this word was spoken, it was spoken under the old covenant. Therefore, the phrase *shall make you* referred to a promise and not a statement of fact. It was something those under the old covenant had to look forward to. But for us the New Creation believers, being the head and not the tail is part of our inheritance in Christ. That's what we are now! Praise God! Something I'd also like you to look at in the sentence structure of this verse. Notice that it says *the* head and not *a* head or a part of it. This means that we are *not* one of many heads, but we are *the* head-the main one. In other words, all other heads are not heads; they are liars and a counterfeit. You need to be conscious of this reality. In Christ Jesus, we have been made *the* head and not the tail. It's obvious that when you say that, you automatically know that you can never be a failure in life. You are married to success for life. Glory to God!

Being *the head* also signifies *ruling* and *reigning* in life. In order to rule or reign, you must be an authority such as a king, priest, president, governor, judge, police, etc. The Bible says in *Revelation 5:10 KJV*, "…

and hast made us kings and priests: and we shall reign on the earth." This is a glorious truth! You and I are kings and priests. We have the power to rule and reign because we are *the head.* Halleluiah!

The scripture also says we are *"above only and not beneath".* This makes me so excited because I often hear some people and any even a few Christians say it's all right for a Christian to be poor. Emphatically No! Did you see what it says? It says *above only!* Meaning there should be no room for poverty, sickness, debts, divorce, lack, misfortune, unproductiveness, shame, sin, and struggling in the life of the Christian. We live above only and nothing less! Beloved, God has given us the higher life to live in Christ. You will live a life of victory everyday of your life when you come to full understanding of who you are in Christ. No longer should you look down on yourself; for God has made you the head. As a Christian, you take charge over every domain of life.

Also, as *the* head and someone living above *only,* you are a person of greater influence. You don't let people or circumstances influence you in the wrong or negative way. I hear that peer pressure is one of the thriving issues young people face in our schools today, and how they are being influenced by friends to do the wrong things. This should not be so for a child of God. You should be of greater influence to your friends or peers. Let your light so shine before them. Let them recognize that you are in charge. You do so by being early to class, making A's, being respectful and courteous to others and preaching to them about Christ. If you don't do these things, you'll become ineffective in your Christian life and as result, you'll become influenced by their bad behaviors. Always be conscious of what you are and who you are in Christ and you will never live under but above only.

Be of greater influence at your work place, at your school, in your family, in your community, with your unit of friends everywhere you are and anywhere you go. Be the one that others look up to and come to for advice. Refuse to always take the back seat of life. You were born [that is when you got born-again] to be influential and you are well advanced. You are not the tail neither are you average in this life; you are the head and above only. You reign in life! Praise God! I charge you to know that you are more than what you think you are and you have been called to reign in this life.

Supporting Scripture(s):

For if because of one man's trespass (lapse, offense) death reigned through that one, much more surely will those who receive [God's] overflowing grace (unmerited favor) and the free gift of righteousness [putting them into right standing with Himself] reign as kings in life through the one Man Jesus Christ (the Messiah, the Anointed One). Romans 5:17 AMP

EXCERPT 23

Who is the Christian?

Hello! A lot of Christians have been misguided by the world's concept of who the Christian is. Nowadays, it seems difficult to distinguish a Christian from a non-Christian. It is because a lot of Christians still don't know who the Christian is suppose to be and as a result they live below who they really are. As a child of God you must know who the Christian is in order to function rightly. It is essential every Christian knows what Christianity is, or we will live by the label or theory the world gives Christianity. As you would know, the world has its interpretation of Christianity is to them, and many of these views are inaccurate with what the Gospel of Christ really teaches.

Christianity is NOT a religion or some sort of religious practice! What is religion? Religion is the belief in a higher power: an institution to express belief in a divine power. In Christianity, believing in a higher power is the lesser included in the greater. It is just a one and lesser part of whole truth. Christianity is more than just believing in a divine power. *Christianity is a relationship and a Life!*

First, what do I mean by Christianity is a relationship? Religion teaches a belief in a higher power; however in religion, there is no relationship with the one in whom they believe in. But, in Christianity, you have a relationship with the God you believe. Your relationship with God is more real than your natural relationships with a parent, a best friend or any other human being on earth. This God is our father and we are His children! We have been translated from servants to son-ship and we have a relationship with Him.

"⁴But when the fullness of the time was come, God sent forth his Son, made of a woman, made under the law, ⁵To redeem them that were under the law, that we might receive the adoption of sons. ⁶And because ye are sons, God hath sent forth the Spirit of his Son into your hearts, crying, Abba, Father. ⁷Wherefore thou art no more a

servant, but a son; and if a son, then an heir of God through Christ."
Galatians 4:4-7 KJV

Secondly, I said Christianity is a Life. You see, animals have the animal life [nature]; humans have the human life, and Christians also, have *the eternal life*-in the Greek this life is called *Zoe*, which means *the God kind of life*. This is the *life* that is in Jesus Christ and everyone who receives Him, receives that same *life*. See 1 John 5:11-13 (KJV). Now Christianity is the life of Jesus Christ manifesting or operating in a person. Christianity is a union with deity [the God life] or deity in humanity.

However, who then is the Christian? Before I continue to share with you on who the Christian is, I'd like to first of all define who the Christian is not. The Christian is **not** the one who goes to church [or a church attendee], although it is part of the Christian walk. The Christian is **not** the one who is born into a Christian family or whose parents are Christians. You can be born in a Godly family and still not be a Christian because to become a Christian is personal and you and only you must ask Jesus Christ into your heart.

The Christian is not the ordinary human being; although he was born as a human being. When you become a Christian, you receive a new nature-the divine nature of God. The Bible says in *2 Corinthians 5:17 KJV* that, *"...If any man be in Christ, he is a new creation..."* In other words, the Christian is **not** an *old* creation [with the ordinary human nature]; he is a *new* creation [with God's own divine nature]. You have to understand that you are no longer the person your mother gave birth to; you are now a new man in Christ. You have God's DNA in you now. Yes you still have a human body, but the human spirit or nature doesn't exist anymore because you have been born again. Old things are truly passed away! That's why the Bible says we are partakers [sharers] of His divine nature. See 2 Peter 1:4 (KJV). When you become conscious of this, you'll see your Christian life in a whole new light.

Furthermore, many have been led to believe that the Christian is an imitation or imitator of Christ. The reality is the Christian is NOT an imitation or imitator of Christ. It is important that we look at meanings of certain words before we begin to use them to describe who we are. I took the liberty to look up some definitions of the word "imitator". I was shocked by what I discovered. An imitator is someone who fraudulently assumes the appearance of another, a fake, caricature, artificial, counterfeit, and not original. These definitions troubled me as read them and I said, "This can't possibly be the truth about who the Christian is". How can the Christian be a fake version, not original or a counterfeit of Christ? That doesn't seem right! Then I remembered one powerful scripture that opened my eyes to who the Christian truly is...

Galatians 2:20 KJV declares, *"I am crucified with Christ: nevertheless I live; yet not I, but Christ liveth in me..."* Paul the Apostle said, he is crucified with Christ and even though he lives, it is not he, but Christ who lives in him. Therefore, the Christian is the one, who is living the *life* of Christ—*Zoe*—the God kind of life; who has allowed Christ to live through him or her. This is vital! As a Christian, you are not an imitation or imitator (remember the definitions) of Christ neither are you trying to copy Him. You now have His very Life in you and you are to live that life as though it was Christ Himself living it on earth. Oh Glory! Many Christians don't know this. They still think they are trying to imitate or copy Christ. I see some Christians when they face a situation; they use this popular phrase "what would Jesus do" (WWJD). The question should not be what would Jesus do? Remember you have His very life in you, so you don't need to stop and think of what Jesus would have done to do the right thing, you should just function according to His life that's in you.

Let's assume a human being was given an animalistic nature. This human who now has an animalistic nature doesn't need to think or ask what an animal will do in a given situation to behave like an animal. He will simply function as an animal because he now has the nature of an animal in him and will naturally live like an animal. This is what it means by being a Christian. You naturally live the life of Christ in you without imitating or asking what He would do, because, now that's your life! As a Christian, you have the life of Christ and that life naturally flows out of you. The life of Christ is not an outside force from the Christian; it is inherent in every Christian. It's in you all the time, whether you realize it or not. So since Christ lives in you, the question is, what would you do?

I pray that your eyes will be enlightened by this wonderful truth to know who the Christian really is. So now, begin to live *conscious* of this truth. Don't try to imitate Christ; be the Christ people can see. When the world looks at you, let them see Christ. If they are still seeing you, know that you have not started living the Christian life yet. But if they can see Christ in you, know that you are living the actual Christian life. I encourage you to search through the Word of God and find out more about who the Christian really is so you can know how you ought to function.

Supporting Scripture(s):

For neither is circumcision [now] of any importance, nor un-circumcision, but [only] a new creation [the result of a new birth and a new nature in Christ Jesus, the Messiah].

Galatians 6:15 AMP

EXCERPT 24

You are a carrier of His presence

✝

Hello! It is of utmost importance that Christians should have the consciousness of God's presence in their lives. Many have taken God's presence to be an outside reality: as something they only experience once in a while or when they are in church or just when they're praying. I've heard too many believers say things like, "Lord, I come into your presence or when I go into the presence of God (referring when they go to pray or spend time with God)." The question I'd like to ask is **where have you been?** The Christian does not come in and out of God's presence. The presence of God is where you live.

When you got born again, you were born into God's presence. In other words, when you receive Christ, you come into a union with the Father and He makes His presence available to you and in you through the Holy Spirit. Therefore, everyone who is born-again lives in and carries God's presence.

Under the old covenant (as in those who lived from Adam to before the resurrection of Christ), the children of Israel only experienced the presence of God as an outside entity. God's presence was with them and not in them. Also, they did not experience the life [nature, glory] of God fully. What I mean by that is, they only experienced His presence occasionally or just for a short time. The Bible says in the book of **Genesis 3:8** that when God had made Adam, He would come and *visit* him at the cool of the day. That word 'visit' implies that He would come and go. The reason I believe it was a visit is because in that same verse it say Adam and Eve hid themselves from the presence of the Lord, meaning God's presence wasn't always there. And in the next verse, God was looking for Adam because He said "Adam, Where art thou?" So God was not in man yet, howbeit man was created in the image and likeness of God.

Before Jesus came and died, buried and was resurrected, those who were under the old covenant (as in those who lived from Adam to before the resurrection of Christ), only experienced the presence of God occasionally or momentarily for specific purposes. However, in Christ (that is after the resurrection of Christ), His presence is not only with us [the believers] all the time, but also in us forever through the Holy Spirit. In other words, the resurrection of Jesus Christ from the dead made it possible for anyone who believes and accepts Jesus, to have the indwelling of the presence [life, nature, glory] of God. That life is what makes you a born again.

In addition, God's presence is now your dwelling place and you have become a carrier of His presence. Hallelujah! It gets better:

'**16** *And I will ask the Father, and he will give you another Advocate, who will never leave you.* **17** *He is the Holy Spirit, who leads into all truth. The world cannot receive him, because it isn't looking for him and doesn't recognize him. But you know him, because he lives with you now and later will be in you.* **18** *No, I will not abandon you as orphans—I will come to you.* **19** *Soon the world will no longer see me, but you will see me. Since I live, you also will live.* **20** *When I am raised to life again,* *you will know that I am in my Father, and you are in me, and I am in you. John 14:16-20 NLT*

In this portion of Scripture, we see that Jesus promised us the Holy Spirit-*the conveyor of God's divine presence*-the one who makes the presence of God available to the Christian. There are a few other things to note in this passage. Firstly, Jesus said to His disciples the Holy Spirit cannot be received of the world because they don't recognize Him and that they [the disciples] have seen Him because He is with them and will *later be in them*. Later there as **verse 20** explains, speaks of when Christ has resurrected, the Spirit of God [the Holy Ghost] will come into them and live in them forever. Since Jesus was speaking to His disciples, that means the Holy Spirit is only given to the believer and not the unbeliever.

I have heard of people who say that when a Christian commits a sin, the Holy Spirit leaves him or her and comes back after he or she has repented of that sin. That's not true and that's not accurate with what the Bible teaches. The Holy Spirit [the one who makes the presence of God available to the believer] didn't come into you because you did something right; therefore,

He doesn't leave you because you did something wrong. In fact, He is there for that purpose; to help you do right. If He leaves you, how will you ever do right? In verse 16 of John 14, Jesus said, the **Holy Spirit will never leave you**, meaning He is in you forever! That means He will never go away. He's there for life! Therefore, if the Christian has the Holy Ghost forever, he or she has *the presence* of God in him or her forever. Dear friend, you carry God in you all the time. This must be your consciousness wherever you are or wherever you go.

In the book of *Exodus 33:15*, Moses said to God, *"...If thy presence go not with me, carry us not up hence."* This means at the moment and before he prayed that prayer, the presence of God was not with him completely because he said, *"if I go not with your presence go not with me."* That show's that he did not have the presence of God in him or with him all the time. I used to pray this prayer too because I thought it sounded spiritual and right. But now I know that the Christian-the one in Christ, who is born-again, is not suppose to pray in that manner because it would mean that he or she is not conscious of the *ever-abiding* presence of God with and in him/her already. Moses could pray like this because in his dispensation, they didn't have the presence of God in them or with them perpetually. God's presence was with them only on specific occasions and many could go for years without ever experiencing the tangibility of God's presence. No wonder, many of them had difficulties following God's precepts and died without entering into God's rest. The dispensation that we live in now is one where, the Christian carries and lives in the presence of God twenty-four-seven, because the Holy Ghost is in you forever.

With this spectacular revelation in mind, you ought to start living differently and consciously of the greater one in you: for greater is he that is in you, than he that is in the world. Glory to God! Imagine if this is your everyday consciousness, how can you ever live in fear, worries, sickness, disease, poverty or sin? Never; not even for one day! Remember, where the Spirit [presence] of the Lord is, there is liberty—*freedom*. Know that God's presence in you is your certificate for a better life. Therefore, walk boldly and always expect the best out every situation you encounter for the Greater One lives in you. I want you to know that you carry God's presence wherever you go; in your school, at your job, in your office, in the market place, at your church, when you are driving, sleeping, working, eating or talking, the presence of God is with and in you. That is why He say's I will never leave you now forsake you. See Hebrews 13:5 (KJV).

This is why we are so highly favored and blessed because we carry His divine presence. You wonder why you drive on the same road, at the same time and someone else has an accident and you don't. Flu season comes around and everybody in your house, class or work gets it and you don't. Everyone goes to apply for the same job and doesn't get it but when you show up, they give it to you and pay you more than you expected. These can only be possible to those who carry the presence of God and are conscious of His mighty presence in them. With the presence of God in you, nothing can be withheld from you! Hallelujah! I urge you by His Spirit to never be afraid or shaken by people or circumstances; remain conscious of the fact that you are a carrier of His presence.

Supporting Scripture(s):

Know ye not that ye are the temple [house, home, carrier] of God, and that the Spirit of God dwelleth in you? 1 Corinthians 3:16 KJV

EXCERPT 25

How to edify your spirit

✝

Hello! It is paramount as a child of God that you focus on things that will edify your spirit. Just like the body, the spirit needs to be fed daily and with the right kind of food to keep it functioning properly. More and more believers today are only concerned about their physical wellbeing and forget about the upkeep of their spirit. Many also feed their spirit with the wrong things and make it difficult for their spirit to be active at all times. For example, if you eat food main for animals, you may experience some type of stomach problems or negative effects because that kind of food is not main for a human body.

There are things you can say or do as a Christian that can diminish the effectiveness of the spirit and give you problems because those things are not meant for your spirit. You can't edify your spirit listening to corruptive music, having a negative attitude, insulting or mocking others, hanging out with the wrong company, watching immoral pictures or videos, laughing at dirty jokes, reading books or articles about witches or that glorifies the devil. Living this way will have a negative impact on your spirit and your life in general.

In *3 John 1:2 KJV*, the Bible says, *"Beloved, I wish above all things that thou mayest prosper and be in health, even as thy soul [spirit] prospereth."* In other words, the prosperity of your life and body is directly proportional to the prosperity of your spirit. It seems that the writer wants us to know that, what it's most vital to a man is the condition of his spirit. If your spirit is strong, automatically everything else that concerns you will be strong as well. But if your spirit is weak, everything else that concerns you will follow suit. Therefore your spirit as a Christian, must be continually nourished, enriched, and edified to maintain effectiveness. For you to edify your spirit, you must constantly apply the following…

1. Meditate on the Word of God: when you meditate on God's Word, it will stir you up and keep you conscious of who you are and what has been made available to you in Christ Jesus.

2. Speak forth God's Word all the time: You become what you speak and if you don't speak, you sleep. One of the evidence that someone is alive and awake is that they speak. Your speaking will keep your spirit from sleeping. Continue to declare what God has said about you.

3. Tame your tongue: Choose your words carefully and let them be seasoned with salt. (Colossians 4:6)

4. Have a joyful countenance: Joy is a fruit of your spirit and you must continue to exercise that joy. When you keep a sad and worrisome demeanor, you lose your willingness to do anything positive and shut down your spirit. This hinders the flow of the God-life in you.

5. Worship and praise: Always be in the mood of worship for it tunes your spirit to God and stirs up your desire to fellowship with Him. Worshiping and praising draws your spirit closer to the throne room of God and makes you more aware of His presence in you and around you.

6. Speak in tongues often: *1 Corinthians 14:4 KJV* says, *"He that speaketh in an unknown tongue edifyeth himself..."* The word *edify* in the Greek is translated, to energize, embolden, build up, charge up, stir up. Speaking in other tongues will do all these things to your spirit and condition it rightly.

7. Surround yourself with Godly people: Notice when you stay near people who smoke for some time, when you leave their presence you will smell like cigarettes even though you may have never touched a cigarette. Just surrounding yourself with negative people is similar to second-hand smoking; in the same way, I've noticed when I get in the company of other strong believers my spirit become more pumped up and energized unto godliness. The Bible says that when Saul, who was very evil and disobedient to God came into a company of prophets, he too began to prophesy. Why? Because he came under that atmosphere of Godly men. See 1 Samuel 19:19-24 (NLT). Your spirit will also become charged when you surround yourself with spiritual folks and stay under a Godly atmosphere.

I challenge you to seek to edify your spirit and keep it in an adequate condition all the time and your will begin to see marvelous changes in your attitude and evidently in your life.

Supporting Scripture(s):

[18]*And do not get drunk with wine, for that is debauchery; but ever be filled and stimulated [edified] with the [Holy] Spirit.* [19]*Speak out to yourself in psalms and hymns and spiritual songs, offering praise with voices [and instruments] and making melody with all your heart to the Lord,* [20]*At all times and for everything giving thanks in the name of our Lord Jesus Christ to God the Father.*[21]*Be subject to one another out of reverence for Christ.*

Ephesians 5:18-21 AMP

CONCLUSION

My prayer for you is that you will continue to meditate on these excerpts and keep them in your remembrance. Also that you become stronger, efficient and more effective in your walk with God. I know that you have received divine insights from this book that will take your spiritual life and walk with God to the next level. Remember that wisdom is the rightful application of knowledge; therefore, put the knowledge you have received from this book to practice. Even after you finish reading this book, again and again so you do not lose the soundness of the understanding you've received. The Word of God always multiplies itself; the more you read it the more you become conscious of it and the power of the Word intensifies. May the Lord grant you divine understanding in the knowledge of Him so you can live the life He has made available for you in Christ Jesus. I trust that you will continue to live every day for Christ and make every day of your life count for Him. Thank you and remain a blessing. Shalom…